America's
Trail of Tears
A Story of Love and Betrayal

By
Dean W. Arnold

ᏣᎳᎩ

CHATTANOOGA
HISTORICAL FOUNDATION CO.

2005

Title: America's Trail of Tears: A Story of Love and Betrayal
(Former title: Cherokee Betrayal: From the Constitution to the Trail of Tears)
Copyright: Dean W. Arnold, 2005
ISBN: 0-9749076-0-X
Cover: Eric Wertz, Jobim Aragon; Typesetting: Eric Wertz
Printing: Blair Digital, Chattanooga, Tennessee

To purchase more copies at $19.95 (+$3 shipping & handling), contact:

Dean Arnold
P.O. Box 2053
Chattanooga, TN 37409
Telephone: (423)-595-3621; (423)-517-8329
E-mail: dean@cdc.net

CD audio book price (under title *Cherokee Betrayal)* is $17.95 + $3 s/h.
(Make all checks payable to Dean Arnold).

America's Trail of Tears

CONTENTS

To Hal and Pat

PROLOGUE

You must cross over a barbed wire fence to reach the spot where one of the greatest Indian chiefs in history was assassinated 165 years ago. Several gunmen shot him in his saddle while his horse took a rest and a drink.

The large flat rock next to a wide, flowing creek is only a few feet from the two-lane highway and is mostly hidden from sight by a cluster of trees at the edge of a forest.

A descendent of one of the chief's colleagues showed me the exact spot after driving me there from her home in the Cherokee Nation.

The crime scene is a about a mile into Arkansas from Northeast Oklahoma. The site is not marked. Perhaps this is because many people, even today, question whether the action was a crime. His grave was also left unmarked for 100 years.

The governor of Georgia called him "the noblest specimen I ever saw of an Indian." Sam Houston, who deliberated with him in the halls of Congress, said his genius and native intellect were inferior to no one.[1]

He was revered by the Cherokees for his ability to see far into the distance. His descendents believe he saved their people from extinction. But even today, the wisdom of his leadership in the events leading to the Trail of Tears remains a mystery—to those few who know the story. Most do not.

This retelling of that grand story starts, not in the heart of the former Cherokee lands of Appalachia—the Carolinas, Georgia, and Tennessee. It begins in a small New England town.

CHAPTER ONE

THE SECRET

John's eye for Sarah, a pretty blonde, age fourteen, would not have been risky under ordinary circumstances. John was a top scholar at a New England school and the son of wealthy parents, desirable qualities for a suitor in the early 1820s. Sarah's age was not a factor in those days, especially if the wedding waited until she was fifteen or sixteen.

Plus, John was no ordinary student. He had already extensively studied rhetoric, surveying, ecclesiastical and common history, three books in the *Aeneid*, two orations of Cicero, and natural philosophy, according to a letter his instructor had written to a Yale professor. He was chosen by school officials to write a letter to President James Monroe. With it they sent a sophisticated calculation of a lunar eclipse developed by John's first cousin, Buck, who was also proficient in the same subjects.

John was tall with black hair that tended to wave. One woman described him as "beautiful in appearance, very graceful, a perfect gentleman everywhere." He was so light-skinned he might have passed for a white man.

And that was the other reason John was no ordinary student in the eyes of Sarah's parents or the school officials. John Ridge was an Indian, son of a famous Cherokee chief, "the Ridge."

How prepared were the citizens of Cornwall, Connecticut, and the trustees of the Cornwall Mission School for a union between an Indian and a white girl? Uncertainty on that question had kept John from telling anyone about his love for Sarah, including Sarah.

But John felt confident from their conversations and interaction that she also loved him. Sarah served as nurse for his scrofulous condition, a skin disorder that affected his hip. The doctors feared it could take his life. During his bed rest, the Northrups, caretakers for the school, appointed their fourteen-year-old daughter to care for the young scholar in the midst of their many duties for the mission school.

The doctor noticed John's remarkable recovery, and, perhaps with a suspicion of the cause, told Mrs. Northrup to look into it. "John now has no disease about him," he said. "But he has some deep trouble and you must find out what it is."[1]

Meanwhile, John's father, after receiving news of his son's threatening illness, had embarked on the long journey to New England from his Cherokee homeland between central Georgia and the Tennessee border at Chattanooga. The Ridge had fought as a young man under the great warrior chief Dragging Canoe, the Indian most feared by the newly formed United States of America. President Washington finally signed the Hopewell Treaty with the followers of Dragging Canoe after the chief's death in 1792.

Although the treaty caused the Ridge's people to give up millions more acres of land—their nation had diminished by two-thirds in several decades—they clung to the clear promise in Article Seven: "The United States solemnly guarantee to the Cherokee Nation, all their lands not hereby ceded."

The treaty also called for the Cherokees to "be led to a greater degree of civilization, and to become herdsmen and cultivators, instead of remaining in a state of hunters."

No Cherokee better modeled the transformation from hunter to cultivator than the Ridge. A tall and muscular warrior who had killed many men during wartime, he now operated a several-hundred-acre plantation where he grew apples, peaches, corn, and cotton, and raised horses, cattle, and hogs.

The Ridge was one of the wealthiest of his people, but even the average Cherokee in his day owned a plow and spinning wheel and grew corn and raised hogs, cattle, and horses. The nation had a number of blacksmiths, weavers, and millers, and they lived in log houses or even brick homes, not wigwams.

And although they had exceeded any other Indian nation in their efforts to comply with Washington's treaty, they continued to be pressured from every side by settlers and frontiersman hungry for more land. Federal agent R. J. Meigs owned a map with which he identified 1,000 intruders on Cherokee land. He called them "shrewd and desperate characters" holding barbarous sentiments toward Indians.[2]

Many of those settlers used as their excuse the fact that the Indian tribes had aligned themselves with the British in the War of 1812. To drive off the Native Americans was to provide a service for the country.

However, the Cherokees were an exception. They voted as a nation to align with the United States. And the Ridge served as an officer with General Andrew Jackson in his campaign against the Creek warriors called "Redsticks." From that time onward he referred to himself as Major Ridge.

General Jackson did a poor job, however, of remembering his Cherokee friends after the war. In the 1817 Jackson Treaty, millions of acres in the Alabama territory were given over to squatters who had illegally settled there.

Jackson had since joined those who believed wholesale removal of tribes to the West was the best solution to the "Indian Question," and was incensed when President Madison ordered the Alabama land returned. However, the indomitable Jackson continued to fight for the area and continued to pressure Cherokees on every front to sign a treaty of removal.

Though Major Ridge spoke no English, he saw the need for his children and the next Cherokee generation to be educated like the whites. Evidently, the Ridge was able to foresee that the upcoming political and legal wars faced by the Cherokees could only be fought by a generation equipped for such battles.

John Ridge felt that tremendous pressure from his parents—the weight of an entire culture's hopes—as he considered whether to confide to his father the undying love he felt in his heart for Sarah. The matter had the potential to cut short his tenure at Cornwall. He also knew his parents, both proud Cherokees interested in promoting their traditions, had their own plans for him to marry a chief's daughter someday.

In excitement, the New Englanders prepared themselves to see a "Prince of the Forest." But when Major Ridge entered the Connecticut community, they weren't prepared for the sight. The chief rented a coach and four for his

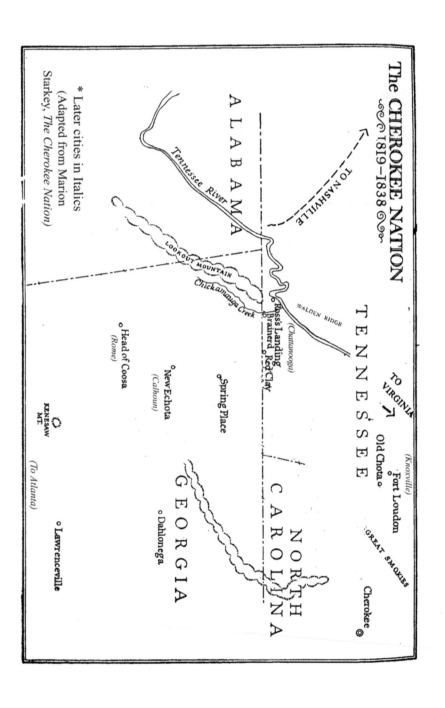

The CHEROKEE NATION
1819–1838

* Later cities in Italics
(Adapted from Marion
Starkey, The Cherokee Nation)

TO NASHVILLE

ALABAMA

Tennessee River

LOOKOUT MOUNTAIN

Chickamauga Creek

WALDEN RIDGE

Ross's Landing
(Chattanooga)
Brainerd Red Clay

Head of Coosa
(Rome)

New Echota
(Calhoun)

Spring Place

KENESAW
MT.

Lawrenceville

(To Atlanta)

TENNESSEE

TO VIRGINIA

(Knoxville)
Fort Loudon
Old Chota

GREAT SMOKIES

NORTH
CAROLINA

GEORGIA

Dahlonega

Cherokee

entry, "the most splendid carriage that ever entered the town." He was a large, tall man in white boots and a coat trimmed with gold.

The future town historian was so taken by the chief that "no memory in my boyhood is clearer than [the visit] of Major Ridge, the Cherokee chief" in his U.S. officer's uniform. "I was impressed with his firm and warlike step. . . I called him the 'nice, big gentleman.' My father exchanged presents with him, giving him a small telescope and receiving in turn an Indian pipe carved in black stone, with the assurance that it had often been smoked in Indian councils."[3]

As father and son spent time together after the initial festivities, it was the perfect opportunity for John to share his real concerns.

To propose something a bit unorthodox or untraditional would not have been out of character for John. When his father had first placed him and Buck in a mission school back in the Cherokee Nation, his cousin had developed that quality so important to missionaries which they called "piety." But John showed "a colder, more calculating manner" and skepticism for the gospel story.

When the two star pupils were moved to the Chickamauga Mission in Chattanooga (later called Brainerd Mission[*]), John was described as "thoughtful."

*Named after David Brainerd, son-in-law to Jonathan Edwards, who ministered to Native Americans in New England 100 years earlier and died at age 27.

However, trouble hit when John, who had already memorized the catechism, was told along with the rest of the class who had missed several spelling words, to study a shorter lesson. John retorted "in a hasty and petulant manner" that he would only study the larger size lesson. "It was spoken in such a way that it could not be passed over," said the missionary, and John was reprimanded.

The news of this rebellious attitude caused Major Ridge to travel sixty miles to address the problem. But John had broken down in tears after the incident, enough to convince the missionaries he was truly sorry. "We could freely forgive him," they said.

The Ridge was elated to hear all was well. He left with an admonition to John: "You must obey them as you would me."[4]

A few months later, John and Buck received the honor of being chosen by the missionaries to attend Cornwall, the prestigious mission school in New England, where students from as many as ten tribes attended, some from as far away as Hawaii. The instructor there, Reverend Herman Daggett, commended Buck for his seriousness, but noted that the intelligent John "refrained carefully from any profession in the Savior."

Later, Rev. Daggett complained of a school wide downward spiral: "I endeavor to use every means to instruct, counsel, and restrain: but unsanctified nature will act like itself." He even noted that Buck was slipping from his pious reputation.

When John and Buck attended the First Church for two sermons each Sunday, they and the other mission students had the opportunity to be in the same proximity as the girls of Cornwall. The boys, however, were restricted to one far corner, "perhaps the same far corner," says Ridge biographer Thurman Wilkins, "in which the back of a gallery pew recorded a critical evaluation of the young man who had recently become the assistant principal:

> The eloquence of Herman Vaill
> Would make the stoutest sinner quail.

The couplet was followed by another of firm dissent:

> The hissing goose has far more sense
> Than Vaill with all his eloquence. "

But apparently Instructor Daggett's hopes were restored a few months later, in part, perhaps, because of John's inclination to verse that included God-fearing allusions. One, entitled "On the Shortness of Human Life," contained an eerie glimpse of his own fate:

> Like as a damask Rose you see,
> Or like the blossom on the tree,
> Or like the morning to the day,

Or like the Sun, or like the Shade,
Or like the Gourd which Jonas had:
Even such is MAN! Whose thread is spun,
Drawn out and cut, and so, 'tis done.
Withers the Rose, the bosom blasts,
The flower fades, the morning hastes,
The sun is set, shadows fly,
The gourd consumes, — so mortals die.

After his sister Nancy died suddenly at age 16, John wrote to his mother: "You know I have been careless about my soul. Yet that great God has not taken me away, as he did my sister. I have abundant reason to thank him for it. Truly it is my desire that He would show me my bad heart and make me feel it."

Although he never claimed a conversion, his instructors were pleased with John and other students who "entertain a hope in Christ." And Buck, Rev. Daggett proudly observed, "is promising both as to piety and to learning."[5]

But it was his own romance, not Buck's, that John needed to tell his father about. Major Ridge, who also had a history of boldly defying inflexible cultural traditions, would likely have sympathized with his son. But there is no record of the two discussing the matter before the chief left Cornwall.

It was left to Sarah's mother, Mrs. Northrup, to confront the troubled Cherokee youth, on the instructions of Dr. Gold. She chose John's room to iron the socks. Eventually she confronted him.

According to the best account given by Sarah's cousin, Ellen Gibbs, Mrs. Northrup said: "You know you have no mother here, only me, and you have always confided in me as you would your mother," she said. "John, you have some trouble and you must tell me," she said.

"No!" said John in defiance. He insisted there was no trouble.

She waited patiently. Then he relented.

"If you must know, I love your Sarah."

She replied, "You mustn't."

"I know it," he said, "and that is the trouble."

"Have you mentioned it to her?"

"No, we have not said one word to each other. I dare not. But how could I help loving her when she has taken such good care of me these two years?"

Mrs. Northrup left to find Sarah. As soon as the young girl came home, she asked her: "Sarah, do you love John Ridge?"

The young lady, who would later prove her self-confidence under testing, answered her mother directly.

"Yes, I do love John."

According to the account, "Mrs. Northrup saw there was trouble in the camp and took Sarah to her grandparents in New Haven and told them to make parties and introduce her to other gentlemen, and try every way to get her mind off John Ridge."[6]

Chapter Two
The Mission

A missionary at Brainerd said he enjoyed taking walks with the Ridge and talking about various subjects, such as geography and astronomy. He was impressed with the intelligent responses.

Certainly the great chief had many times visited the central geographical spot of the region and looked out from the rock at the point of Chatanuga Mountain, later called Lookout. To his right he could view the heart of the Cherokee Nation, a day's journey south into Georgia. As a young chief he could see the unmarked river before him, the mighty Tenasee, flowing from the east near Chickamauge Creek, where the mission, the first white settlement, would eventually be located. That river curved around the bottom of the point of Chatanuga Mountain in the shape of a foot, forming Moccasin Bend.

At the age of five, he floated by canoe past this same creek and mountain when his father moved the family, fearing danger, from the Hiawassee area to the Walden Mountain.* His father later taught him how to walk without noise, and how to mimic the cry of the fawn to attract

*Present-day Signal Mountain, in Tenesee.

the deer.

He knew these mountains well, as his name indicated. In childhood he was called "He who slays the enemy in the path" or the "Pathkiller." But as a teenager he developed a reputation as a great hunter and would tell those at the camp who asked where he returned from, "I came along the top of the mountain."

So the people gave him a new name—not an uncommon practice—pronounced Kah-nung-da-tla-geh, "The man who walks on the mountaintop." To the whites, he was the Ridge.

The first white missionaries also felt the urge to scale the mountain. "The summit of Lookout Mountain overlooks the whole country," wrote Elias Cornelius, who founded the Chickamauga mission as head of the American Board of Foreign Missions in New England, along with Cyrus Kingsbury, who was first introduced to the Cherokee chiefs by Andrew Jackson in 1817.

It was "a view of an interminable forest, penetrated by the windings of a bold river . . . a landscape which yields to few others, in extent, variety, or beauty."[1]

But it was the intent of this staunchly Calvinistic missionary society, a mixture of Congregationalists and Presbyterians, to transform the wild forest into a cultivated civilization. The small community at Brainerd would be the first fruit toward that effort.

Though General Andrew Jackson was America's most notorious Indian fighter, he also fully supported the efforts to educate and civilize the "savages." During his battle with the fierce Creek Indians during the War of 1812, the complex frontier warrior and Indian antagonist found an abandoned Creek infant that other Creek women planned to kill since the child had lost all relatives. Jackson, who had been orphaned at fourteen, said he felt an unusual sympathy for him.

Then and there, he adopted the child and named him Lyncoya. He sent him back to his wife and two sons. "Charity and Christianity says he ought to be taken care of," he wrote them. But keep him in the house, because "he is a Savage."[2]

Jackson insisted he loved the Indians. He was their greatest friend. Nevertheless, he was now one of America's loudest champions of Indian removal, believing that the native cultures could not survive the relentless advancement of white settlers across the continent. They needed to be removed far west to be given time to civilize without outside interference.

Jackson was a popular hero in the Southern states for his views on the "Indian Question." Americans were participating in the greatest opening up of land in history. The state governments awarded occupancy rights to those who squatted on Indian lands, who in turn would then sell the land again for twice and three times the amount to speculators—who would then make even more on it. State laws unquestionably reinforced the settlers' tendency to build on Indian territory.

At a time when the issue of federal versus states rights had not been resolved, the national government found itself divided between federal treaty promises and the contention of Southern states that they owned the land and the Indians must be removed.

After the Louisiana Purchase of the western lands, President Thomas Jefferson was one of the first to suggest removal as a solution to the problem of a slower-than-expected civilizing process. But in 1808 he told a group of Indians in Washington D.C.: "We shall all be Americans."

"You will mix with us by marriage. Your blood will run in our veins, and will spread with us over this great continent."

"Nothing is so easy as to learn to cultivate the earth. . . . Once you have property, you will want laws and magistrates to protect your property. You will unite yourself to us, join us in our great councils and form one people with us."

The progress of the Cherokees passed Jefferson's standard, but Jackson, who had his own presidential ambitions, wanted no exception to the common vision of one vast, uninterrupted American country.

But did he support Indian schools? Yes. In Jackson's view at the time, continued civilization of the Cherokees would devalue their vast hunting lands and allow for more purchases of the land for settlers. He supported the mission, and introduced the Rev. Cyrus Kingsbury to the chiefs during a council where he was arguing for the 2.2 million acres given without the Cherokees' consent to squatters in Alabama.

Jackson also continued to push for individual Cherokees to emigrate west, agreeing to give every enrollee a rifle, ammunition, a blanket, and a brass kettle "as a full compensation for the improvements which they may leave."[3]

The northern missionaries found themselves in sympathy with the Cherokees' desire to remain, and privately opposed the removal policy while doing their best to remain neutral in public.

"The Indians don't know how to understand the President," wrote Kingsbury to a New England colleague.

"A few years ago he sent them a plough and a hoe and said it was not good for his red children to hunt," wrote Kingsbury. "Now he tells them there is good hunting at the Arkansas (present day Oklahoma). If they go there, he will give them rifles."

Then, remembering that his colleague was affiliated with the *Missionary Herald*, he added, "Perhaps it will be best not to publish the above."

Kingsbury also detested the racism all about the frontier. "You cannot conceive the state of feelings [against them]," he wrote, including the publicly Christian settlers, who insisted that "the Indian is by nature radically different from all other men. This difference presents an insurmountable barrier to his civilization."

The missionaries opposed removal as a question of conscience. "If the attempt should succeed, I should blush for my country," Kingsbury said.

Meanwhile, Elias Cornelius made it clear to the chiefs that the missionaries opposed removal, and that the commissioners of the recent Jackson treaty acted entirely without authority.

Despite their white skin, the missionaries' views on removal and race were strong enough to earn the chiefs' trust. And the New Englanders had the makings of a strategic ally. The Ridge spoke with an interpreter at the council to accept the offer for more mission schools. "He spoke with great animation," said Cornelius, "in a loud tone of voice and in true native style."

The Ridge said it was right to accept their offer. The Cherokees wanted their children to act well, to know their Creator, and to work the land for their living. "I am sensible that the hunting life is not to be depended on."

During his founding visit to the Brainerd Mission in 1817, Cornelius preached a sermon. For his text he chose Jesus' famous words in the Gospel of Matthew: "What shall it profit a man if he gains the whole world, yet loses his own soul?"[4]

In time, Cornelius spotted the two brightest students at the Brainerd mission, John Ridge and Buck Watie, and invited them to attend the prestigious mission school in Cornwall, Connecticut.

But the precocious John had ignited a dangerous spark. Should it kindle into a fire, his passions threatened to destroy the key alliance between the Cherokees and the New England missionaries. And neither party was aware of the smoldering flame.

John Ridge

Major Ridge

CHAPTER THREE
THE SCANDAL

Buck Watie was baptized at the First Church of Cornwall while his first cousin John watched from the pews.

Every spring the mission school put on a public exhibition of their promising young Indians, a big event that required the church building, because no other facility in town was large enough for the crowd.

The students spoke on the stage first in their own tongue, then in English. "The Indian pupils appeared so genteel and graceful on the stage that the white pupils appeared uncouth beside them," wrote church member Ellen Gibbs. "The Indians sang and prayed in their native tongue; when they prayed, they knelt, clasped both hands together and held them up."

Indian students were not allowed to go a certain limit beyond the school, and could not visit anyone's home without an invitation. However, if they publicly professed the Christian faith, they were given a written permit to travel two or three miles for evangelistic purposes.

"We always laid aside our work when the scholars came," said Gibbs. "They talked and prayed from the heart."[1]

Invitations to visit homes in the community often came after church services on Sunday. One of the most popular houses to visit was that of Colonel Benjamin Gold, son of the founding preacher of First Church, Hezekiah Gold, and one of the founders and key benefactors of the mission school.

Hezekiah sent two of his sons to Yale, as did Benjamin Gold. Two of Benjamin's daughters married Congregational ministers.

Colonel Gold was a church deacon and had been a Connecticut legislator. The First Church would often receive a visit from the Rev. Lyman Beecher, the most famous preacher in Connecticut and the visionary founder of the Cornwall School.

During Major Ridge's initial visit, he met with Dr. Beecher, who had recently settled into a more quiet life of farming to quiet his dyspepsia. Beecher talked much about obtaining and clearing his acreage, which soured the Ridge who was wary of any white man who seemed greedy for land.

During these get-togethers at the Golds' where leaders like Beecher attended, the romance of a Cornwall girl with Indian scholar John Ridge, still not a professing Christian, remained a secret. Sarah Northrup was now with her grandparents. Relatives were frantically introducing her to potential suitors.

But Buck was a favorite of Cornwall and the Gold family. He was a remarkable writer and had developed a correspondence with several in town, including two of Colonel Gold's children, Stephen and Harriet. His letter to a mission school donor was so lauded by instructor Daggett that it was published in the *Religious Intelligencer*:

"I am a Cherokee, from a nation of Indians living in the southern part of the United States. There are eight of us here from that nation. Six out of eight profess to be followers of the meek and lowly Jesus. . . . I feel sometimes an ardent desire to return to my countrymen and to teach them the way of salvation. Pray for me that my faith fail not, and that I may not finally prove insincere."[2]

While his cousin could follow perfectly the script of the heathen turned Christian, John found himself agonizing over how or whether to pursue his love for Sarah. He wanted to hear from her. He wanted to hear from his parents and learn how they felt about a mixed marriage.

Most importantly, he wondered how the missionary community would react if his interests became public.

The missionaries and New England Christians were fond of quoting the Bible verse in the book of Acts: "God hath made of one blood all nations." A few missionaries at Brainerd, including the superintendent's son, were married to Cherokee converts. The treaties encouraged intermarriage—as had Washington and Jefferson themselves—and white settlers had been marrying Cherokee women for two centuries.

Despite John's full awareness of his parents' desire for him to lead the nation in the future with the wife of a Cherokee chief's daughter, he wrote his mother asking permission to marry Sally (Sarah's nickname).

A troubled Susanna Ridge showed the letter to her husband, Major Ridge. A Christian convert herself, she also showed the letter to Brainerd missionary Daniel Butrick and asked his opinion.

"I told her that a white woman would be apt to feel above the common Cherokees," Butrick wrote to a colleague. "Her son would promise more usefulness to his people were he connected with them in marriage."[3]

When John received his mother's reply refusing her consent (Cherokee mothers typically held sway in such decisions), it might have been enough for him to end all ideas of upsetting the system. But by that time he was likely aware of the response of Sally who had just moved back from New Haven.

"She stayed three months; would take no notice of any gentlemen, or any company," reported cousin Ellen Gibbs." She lost much weight and turned sickly. "They were alarmed about her and brought her home."

John lost no time in writing his mother again.

"When he described his love for Sarah, his mother relented," wrote historian Thurman Wilkins. "On receiving Susanna's permission, John asked Sarah to marry him. He spoke not in shame or a sense of racial inferiority, for he had been raised in pride of his Cherokee heritage: the men of his generation had fought the whites for generations, and within his own lifetime their performance had equaled that of General Jackson's best white soldiers, the conduct of his own father having been recognized the most valiant of all."[4]

The Northrups, school caretakers, were not high dignitaries of Cornwall and were not originally from the small town. Their daughter had also made no public statement yet about her faith. The parents concluded they were not opposed to the idea of a marriage, particularly to a family as wealthy as the Ridges.

Something had to be done, wrote Gibbs. "John was dying for Sarah and Sarah was dying for John." The issue came down to John's health—the illness kept him hobbling. "Finally, Mrs. Northrup told John to go home and stay two years and if he could come back without his crutches, he might marry Sarah."

Given the status of the Northrups and the two young lovers at Cornwall, the proposed marriage had a chance of causing only a limited stir.

But when the news of the alliance reached Isaac Bunce, editor of the *American Eagle* in nearby Litchfield, Connecticut, John's suspicions were realized.

Bunce, in an article entitled in all caps, "INTERMARRIAGES," wrote of the "affliction, mortification, and disgrace of the relatives of the young woman. . . . To have her thus marry an Indian and taken into the wilderness among savages, must indeed be a heart-rending pang." He identified the true cause of the scandal to be the "Missionary Spirit" and, while choosing not to name the girl or the Indian by name, he did single out church leaders such as Beecher, First Church Pastor Timothy Stone, and instructor Daggett.

Bunce noted that some of the people at Cornwall believed "the girl ought to be publicly whipped, the Indian hung, and the mother drown'd."[5]

The mission school leaders were stunned by the attack. As John headed home to heal, he anxiously waited for reports on how the Christian leaders would respond.

Only one person was more interested than John. His first cousin would be the person most eager to watch the reaction, because the town did not yet know about another blossoming romance. Harriet Gold, nineteen, the "perfectly pious" daughter of Benjamin Gold, had fallen in love with Buck. And the two had expressed to each other privately their desire to marry.

Elias Boudinot (Buck Watie)

Harriet Gold

CHAPTER FOUR
THE LAND

John Ridge headed for his home just south of the Smoky Mountains near Chattanooga on his quest to heal his body and muster enough courage to come back for his bride in New England.

The second half of the trip was by land, but a ship took him to Charleston, South Carolina, first, where he stopped for a time to raise money from those of the sympathetic public to aid his people against the proponents of removal.

On November 6, 1822, he gave a speech at Charleston's Circular Church on the history of the Cherokees. John had heard stories as a child from the tribal prophets and conjurers who clothed themselves in large bird wings as they spoke at the council fire.

A large bird, in fact, accounted for the Cherokee story of creation. The Great Buzzard flew across the muddy earth until it grew tired and its wings began to flap slowly and cause ripples in the land. That area became the mountainous region inhabited by the Ani-Yunwiyah, the Real People.

Before they reached the land of the Great Buzzard's wings, the Real People had lived far, far away—no one knew how far—in a cold, snowy place before migrating to a land where they fought with the Iroquois, a people similar to the Real People. They then moved further south to their present home in the mountains.

While holding council with an Iroquois tribe, the chief one day warned them that he had come from a trip thirteen moons away. There he had found strange men who came from the ocean—white-skinned men the Cherokees came to know as Unakas.

Charleston was a fitting city for John Ridge's talk. It was the first area ceded to the Unakas in a treaty with the Real People. Since that time, they had agreed to another 24 treaties, watching their land shrink to a tenth of its original size.

Notable among the cessions was a tract sold away by Chief Atta Culla-Culla for a cabin full of trade goods. The area consisted of nearly the entire future state of Kentucky.[1]

Land in the New World was widely viewed as every settler's chance to become rich. Many historic fortunes were made in America through land speculation, and Andrew Jackson and President Martin Van Buren were among the many who succeeded. Many thousands more desperately pushed forward into the West to find their fortune, and most succeeded in securing at least the minimum purchase required by the government—640 acres or one square mile—in order to gain a purchase price of $2 per acre. In areas like Alabama, the resale of the land was bid at auction as high as $78 per acre.

By the early 1800s, nearly a third of the Irish nation had crossed the Atlantic in search of land and opportunity. The number of Europeans coming to America doubled almost every five years. According to English historian Paul Johnson, bargain prices for land in the United States led to more people acquiring freehold land during this time than at any time in the history of the world.[2]

The land claimed by the native Americans was used primarily for hunting grounds that were sometimes shared with other tribes. They lived communally in villages where private property lines were not drawn. Whites viewed the vast areas, used only for hunting, as a waste.

The Puritans argued from the beginning that the original inhabitants lost their right to the land by failing to obey the first commandment in Genesis to till and subdue the land. The land was, technically, *vacuum domicilium* (no habitations) and needed godly owners.

"The whole earth. . . . hath been given to the sons of Adam to be tilled and improved by them," wrote Massachusetts Bay Governor John Winthrop in 1629.

"Why then should we stand starving here for the places of habitation. . . . and in the mean time suffer whole countries, as profitable for the use of man, to lie waste without any improvement?"

That's why Winthrop could write about a "wonderful plague" that hit the savages before the colonists arrived. "The Lord Hathe cleared our title to what we possess," he concluded.

Even adamant non-Puritans like Thomas Jefferson held similar views of agrarian idealism. "Those who labor in the earth are the chosen people of God, if ever there were a chosen people," he wrote in 1784.[3]

God's chosen people were forging ahead toward their fortunes and their new promised land. The natives were in the way, but American leaders assured the frontiersmen that treaties with the Indians would continue to open up more land for them, just as had happened in the past. In fact, Jefferson gave Georgia a written promise that they would obtain title to the Cherokee Nation in exchange for Georgia giving up the land that became Alabama and Mississippi. That 1802 treaty would later haunt the Cherokees, whose formal consent was not obtained. But the American leaders were confident that the Indians would eventually consent to giving up their land.

"Few white westerners doubted that these obstacles would be overcome," wrote historian William McLoughlin. "White America seemed convinced that God and natural law had ordained from the beginning that European settlers in the New World, especially those of Anglo-Saxon or Nordic stock, should extend their dominion over the continent from coast to coast."

Leaders like Jefferson knew that the westward expansion could lead to an American empire. Acquiring the land of the frontier had the potential to change the struggling ex-colonies into a major nation.

This commitment to "Manifest Destiny" left the federal government under pressure to continually make treaties with Indians to secure more available land. As the federal government encouraged the Indians to civilize and begin farming, it also encouraged them to purchase supplies and tools and other expensive investments on credit, leading, hopefully, to more land cessions to make the payments. President Jefferson in particular urged storekeepers to keep the Indians in debt so that they would be obliged to agree to land cessions.[4]

If that didn't work, other "inducements" were utilized that looked to the other chiefs like simple bribery, but this was difficult to prove.

Take the case of Doublehead, the leading Cherokee Chief in the early 1800s. His fellow chiefs, including the Ridge, were angry with his agreement to sell their best hunting grounds, which included a large part of Tennessee, Muscle Shoals in Alabama, and parts of Kentucky. They questioned how he developed so much wealth in a short time, including two stables of blooded horses and two dozen slaves who worked his lands. News later leaked out that he had acquired two tracts of land at the mouth of the Clinch and Hiawassee rivers that he rented out to whites. Another had been given to Talohnteskee, Doublehead's relative, at the mouth of the Duck River.

Doublehead was denounced by the council, which decided he should be executed for selling away the nation's lands. The Ridge was chosen for the bloody task, and he found the short but muscular chief sitting as a spectator at a ballplay, the Cherokee's national sporting event in which teams of twelve on both sides used sticks with leather pouches to throw a ball into a goal—the forerunner of lacrosse.

Traditionally, the ballplay included dances by the women and special rites of ceremony and purifying acts of self-denial by the participants, who might later, like some spectators, enjoy relations such as those easily seen in the woods with an unmarried woman. But with the introduction of whiskey, the ballplay had evolved into a more sordid event that the missionaries strenuously condemned.

Doublehead had imbibed in too much whiskey at the ballplay and then began fighting Bone Polisher. Doublehead crushed Bone Polisher's skull with the butt of a pistol. But he was unable to elude a bullet by the Ridge and had his own skull crushed by Alexander Saunders, who assisted the Ridge.

Doublehead's treaty had included land for an ironworks facility where the Chickamauga Creek flowed into the Tennessee River. But the hopeful owner, Elias Earle, had his caravan of supplies stopped by an armed company led by the Ridge and fellow chief David Vann.

"Be careful of Vann's party," Earle wrote to the federal agent, "who, I am convinced, is determined to kill you, if possible."

In fact, the chiefs limited their show of force to the singular incident and no other violence resulted. "The consensus was that, however crudely, justice had been done," said historian Wilkins. "Doublehead's death benefited the Cherokees in a number of ways, including increased tribal unity."

Indeed, a few months later the council—led by such names as Pathkiller, Ridge, Saunders, Young Wolf, Sour

Mush, George Fields, and Sharp Arrow—ruled that the nation would no longer allow any government, federal or state, to treat with only a minority of chiefs. The entire council must approve any land cession.[5]

President James Madison was in no position, however, to address such willfulness by the Cherokees. A larger threat had emerged on the frontier—a call for an alliance of every Native American tribe on the continent against the white man.

The great Shawnee chief Tecumseh had come south to visit the Creeks, his mother's tribe and the Cherokees' neighbors, in the ancient town of Tookabatcha in Alabama. Representatives from all the southern tribes were there to hear his message. For Tecumseh, the only way to survive was to fight. The Unakas could not be defeated at their own game of laws and treaties.

"Let the white race perish," he cried. "They seize your land. They corrupt your women. They trample on the bones of your dead. Back whence they came, on a trail of blood, they must be driven. Burn their dwellings—destroy their stock—slay their wives and children that their very breed may perish!"

Ridge attended the speech with 40 other Cherokee chiefs. But they all chose to defy Tecumseh, deciding instead that they could, indeed, live amid the white man and develop as a nation. They would learn the civilization of the Europeans while also continuing their own traditions. They knew they could not beat the white man, but they believed they could play his game along with him.

Half of the Creek nation did join Tecumseh. But when the others told him they would not, he accused them of having white blood.

"You do not believe the Great Spirit sent me. You shall believe it," he said and then promised to send an earthquake. "I will leave directly and go to Detroit. When I get there I will stamp my foot upon the ground and shake every house in Tookabatcha."[5]

Nevertheless, the Cherokees volunteered their services to the United States against the British in the War of 1812. The Ridge, who as the nation's greatest orator was credited for recruiting 800 warriors to the cause, was designated a major. Other notable soldiers included the Ridge's old friend White Path who had fought with him as a teenager, John Ross, grandson of the first British agent John McDonald who advised Dragging Canoe at Chickamauga Creek, and an odd, more withdrawn Cherokee silversmith named George Gist who could not read or write.

Gist's interaction with the whites during the war inspired his quest to find a way for the Cherokees to obtain their own "talking leaf."

"He was a poor man," John Ridge later wrote, "and he told the head men one day that he could make a book. The chiefs replied it was impossible, because, they said, the Great Spirit at first made a red and a white boy; to the red boy he gave a book, and the white boy came round the red boy, stole his book and went off, leaving him the bow and arrow, and therefore an Indian could not make a book. But George Gist thought he could. He shut himself up to his study."[7]

It would be another decade before Gist's odd ideas were noticed. Meanwhile, he and his colleagues fought under the command of Tennessee General Andrew Jackson. The Ridge had made the acquaintance of the "Hero of New Orleans," whose military feats had made him perhaps the most famous man in America.

But Jackson's obsession with protecting the nation's frontier from European and Indian threats far outweighed any relational ties developed during the war. The friendly Creeks' principal chief, Big Warrior, learned this immediately after the war when the Hero demanded 23 million acres of land from the Creeks—about three-fifths of the state of Alabama. And Jackson demanded four million acres from the Cherokees. Nevertheless, he began by saying to his "Cherokee Children," as he always did before any council, "I am your friend and brother."

When Big Warrior protested in council, Jackson said the U.S. would have been justified by the Great Spirit had they taken all the lands of the nation, because the Creeks had listened to Tecumseh.

No, they had not. They chose not to fight, Big Warrior said. They did the right thing.

If they had done the right thing, Jackson said, they would have seized Tecumseh immediately and delivered him over to the United States as a prisoner. "Or, have cut his throat," he added.

The Creeks felt forced to make the treaty. But the Cherokees refused, and sent a delegation to Washington explaining that the four million acres belonged to them and could not be taken without their consent. Madison agreed and signed a treaty that overruled Jackson's.

Jackson fumed, and wrote the Secretary of War nearly every day, sometimes twice a day, in his determination to defeat the Cherokee treaty.

"The people of the West will never suffer any Indian to inhabit this country again," he wrote. The "hasty and iniquitous" treaty could lead to "the destruction of the whole Cherokee Nation, and of course to a civil war."

But he finally acknowledged the treaty as binding. "We must get clear . . . [of] this hateful instrument," he concluded. The method would be through "just compensation."

He told his subordinate to meet with Pathkiller, the Ridge, and a few other chiefs and have them "resign all claim for a very small sum. They know they never had any right and they will be glad as I believe to swindle the U States out of a few thousand dollars, and bury the claim, if persisted in, which they know might bury them and their nation."[8]

The council, continually fearing that renegade chiefs might take bribes and treat with Jackson, passed a law on July 7, 1818, stating any Cherokee who sold land without approval of the full council would be subject to death. In fact, several were later found to be conspiring with Jackson. When the plot was discovered, they were impeached for treason.

The state of Georgia, fearful of the growing confidence of the Cherokees, convinced Congress to appropriate money toward negotiations that would lead to the extinction of all their 7200 square miles within Georgia—most of the nation.

The Cherokees, alarmed, acted quickly. Judges were appointed for several districts to obtain the sentiment of the entire nation. They reported back to the council: The people were unanimous and determined not to sell, "being resolved not to dispose of even one more foot of ground."

The federal agent, who consulted with Jackson, called the rebuff—and such statements as being a "free and distinct nation"—as "little short of a declaration of independence." It would be a disaster if other tribes followed their lead. "This principle, once established, could be subversive of all order," wrote another agent.[9]

Seeing the danger, but also realizing that "inducements" from fellow natives would be far more effective than from a white man, the agents met with the head of the Creek Nation who was to soon hold council with the Cherokees. They hoped a large enough gift, passing through the hands of a fellow native, would convince the chiefs, finally, to sell and remove.

CHEROKEE TERRITORIAL LOSSES

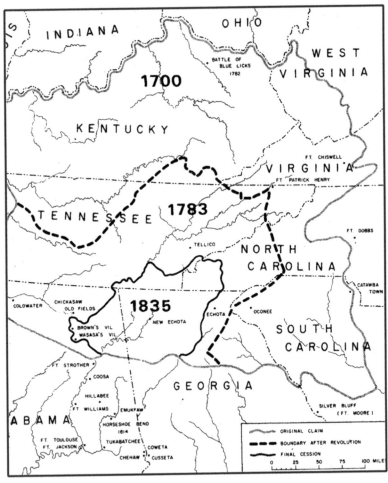

*From William McLoughlin, *Cherokee Renascence.*

CHAPTER FIVE

THE BRIBE

John Ridge and cousin Buck returned from Cornwall to Brainerd Mission as young heroes. John, with his intellect and advanced training, was already considered a leading man of the nation.

Buck was immediately dispatched by the missionaries to aid in riding circuit with a minister. He served as interpreter, spoke before gatherings, and led in prayer. His cousin, who said his hip restricted his movements, stayed home.

John arrived back in the nation just in time to attend, as a prominent leader in the nation, his first legislative council—the council where Chief William McIntosh of the Creek Nation would address the Cherokees. John served as the formal interpreter for this important event.

"I had the first opportunity of acquainting myself with the manner of proceedings," he wrote. At the solemn council, "the whole confidence and talent of the Nation was now seated."

The Council, which served as a senate-like upper house, included John's father, who served as Speaker of the

Council. The venerable Pathkiller was Principal Chief, and the President of the lower house National Committee was the rising leader John Ross. Ross was a short man of only five feet six inches who was also only one-eighth Cherokee. His appearance for all practical purposes was entirely Scottish.

General McIntosh arrived as representative for the Creeks and was hailed as "beloved brother." He was escorted to the White Bench reserved for dignitaries.

In private conversation he told council members he favored a treaty for removal. And then McIntosh chose to approach Ross and told him he would receive $2,000 "for present" if he would favor a treaty.

Ross asked McIntosh to verify the promise in writing. The Creek leader did so willingly. "Nobody shall know about it," McIntosh said.

The next morning both the upper and lower houses met together, and John Ross arose with the letter in his hand. He informed the chiefs that a "gross contempt" had been made of his principles, as well as that of the General Council. "This letter will speak for itself. Fortunately, the author has mistaken my character and my sense of honor."

The Ridge arose to "break" the Creek chief. "As Speaker for the Cherokee Nation," he said, "I depress him. I cast him behind my back. I now divest him of trust." A letter of warning was sent to the Creek Council.[1]

The federal agents, who had bribed McIntosh with $7,000 to persuade the Cherokees, admitted to Secretary of War John C. Calhoun they had been bested. "The Cherokees are far in advance of any other tribe in civilization," they reported.

Calhoun had heard enough. "You must be sensible," he told the chiefs, saying their tendency to act "as a distinct nation within the limits of Georgia or any other state . . . is incompatible with our system." He cited the clause in the Constitution forbidding the creation of new states within a current state without its consent.

Then he wrote a federal agent to warn that the federal government was planning to withdraw its protection of Cherokee borders as outlined by Washington's treaty. "They assume to be an independent people. Let them act up to its spirit," he wrote. "Surrounded as the Cherokees are by the white population, a savage people are doomed when they come into contact with enlightened and civilized nations."[2]

When other arguments failed, the right of conquest by a just war was never far from the debate. As Jackson had earlier told the Cherokees, removal to the West was not an option: "The promise of the President to the Arkansas must be fulfilled," he solemnly warned. "And it *will* be fulfilled."[3]

The leaders of the American Board for Foreign Missions were quite influential in Washington. Some were members of Congress, and their influence lay entirely with the anti-Jackson party. The missionary board had formed a partnership with the federal government, and some of their financial support and most of their buildings came from federal funds.

When Secretary Calhoun received reports that missionaries may be trying to thwart government policy, he demanded an explanation from Cyrus Kingsbury, who was accused of using his influence to prevent the Cherokees from removing.

The missionaries continued to plead innocent to meddling in politics. Kingsbury assured the federal government he had not encouraged the Cherokees against removal.

Under such a cloud John Ridge weighed the question of returning to Cornwall as he watched his hip successfully heal. He had thrown away his crutches as Sarah's mother insisted.

The first fiery editorial by Isaac Bunce—which condemned mixed marriages and blamed the "missionary spirit" for such perversions in Connecticut—caused subscriptions to the *American Eagle* to increase sharply. Bunch immediately wrote another.

"Have not the females in that place been seen to ride and walk out with [the Indian students] arm in arm, by night and by day—spend evenings with them—invite them to tea parties—correspond with them by letters," he wrote, and then he fueled the fire of racism, "while the young men of the town, poor white boys, were often cast into the shade by their colored and tawny rivals?"

The insult caused the young men of the town to meet together and write a resolution: "Resolved: That though we feel no spirit of boasting in this case, and though we do not profess to be 'ladies men,' still we spurn at the intimation that we have been cast into the shade, by our rivals, white or tawny."[4]

Though he was aware of the contentious atmosphere he would be entering, John Ridge decided that he would not be prevented from marrying his beloved Sarah. As he would do later in life, John refused to be pressured into an either/or decision and determined he would use his abilities and creativity to accomplish all his goals. He would marry Sally. He would convince the missionaries, and they would remain an ally in Congress. He would lead his nation into the future.

John and his father left for Cornwall in December of 1823, and he found Sarah more in love with him than before. The news "spread like wildfire" and was condemned from pulpits. But the pastor of the Second Congregational Church was willing to perform the ceremony. According to one observer, "Ridge came near to being mobbed." The Northrups thought it wise for them to leave at once, and they accompanied the newly married couple on the first part of the journey past aroused crowds who learned of the scandal from the papers—"excited throngs denouncing [Ridge] for taking away as a wife—a white girl."[5]

John later admitted that he had won a battle with the whites and "plucked one of its finest flowers." But he refused from the beginning that he was her inferior in any respect.[6]

The sensational romance had the girls of the town writing mythical verse with Indian metaphor that hardly applied to the modern John Ridge:

O, come with me, my white girl fair,

O, come where Mobile's sources flow;

With me my Indian blanket share,

And share with me my bark canoe;

We'll build a cabin in the wild,

Beneath the forest's lofty shade,

With logs on logs transversely piled,

And barks on barks obliquely laid.[7]

The girls were told that Sarah had 30 servants living in the backyard. "She simply said to this one go and he goeth, and to another one come, and he did so. She dressed in silk every day." Perhaps in reaction to this romanticism came the rumors that the union had been caused by an abnormal interest in mixed marriage by Mrs. Northrup.

"Such an excitement had never been seen in town before," wrote Sally's cousin. Editor Bunce added to the fervor with the ominous warning that three other engagements with Indian scholars were in progress.[8]

Eight heads of family at Cornwall decided that Bunce must be answered for his accusations of improper interaction between the scholars and their daughters. One of the letter signers was Colonel Benjamin Gold, father of fourteen children, who himself had two marriageable daughters in town, including nineteen-year-old Harriet.

"For some time past, there have been frequent assertions in the paper . . . that there is a kind of intercourse subsisting between the families in the 'valley of Cornwall' with the 'foreign scholars' which is highly improper," they wrote. "We fully believe they are not facts; we deny that they are facts; and, in our turn, assert that they are base fabrications."[9]

To further protect the image of the mission school and to prevent any more damage, founder Lyman Beecher and school authorities forbade any other marriages across race lines, condemned the idea of mixed marriages in general, and encouraged the Christians of Cornwall to turn their focus back to the saving of souls.

Colonel Gold and his family had never considered mixed marriage as sinful. But that was before Harriet approached her father just days after his defense of the foreign scholars had been published. She asked permission to marry Buck, with whom she had been corresponding regularly. She was "a favorite of the village, and the idol of the family," and she had long held ambitions of becoming a missionary. Now she argued that marrying an Indian from a foreign land put her in the best possible position to reach the heathen for the gospel.

Unlike the alliance of John and Sarah, this proposal involved two publicly professing Christians with impeccable reputations for piety. And to complicate matters, Buck did not share his cousin's lighter complexion. With his high cheekbones and straight black hair, he "looked the Indian" despite his scholarly clothing.[10]

Harriet's parents tried every way to change her mind. Their other daughters had married wealthy men, ministers, lawyers, and judges. "All had married so well, it was a dreadful stroke to have Harriet marry an Indian," reported Gibbs. Ministers from other towns came to talk with her, but she stood firm. "We have vowed, and our vows are heard in heaven," she said. "Color is nothing to me. His soul is as white as mine. He is a Christian and ever since I embraced religion I have been praying that God would open a door for me to be a missionary, and this is the way."[11]

When it was clear she would not change her mind, Colonel Gold acted on his authority as head of the home and forbade the marriage. He sent off a letter to the Indian scholar with the message. Harriet collapsed. The same doctor who attended to John Ridge sought frantically to restore Harriet, who had become deathly ill.

Andrew Jackson

John Ross

CHAPTER SIX:

THE LINGUIST

Buck Watie was born in 1803 in the heart of the Cherokee Nation. His father was Oowatie or "the Ancient One," shortened to Watie. He named his son Gallagina, which translated means "The Buck."

Watie was brother to The Ridge, whose lead he followed in sending his young son to the first mission ever established in the nation, the small German-Moravian school of John and Anna Gambold in Spring Place. The boy soon became their favorite student. When "our promising little Buck" was taken from his teachers to attend the Brainerd school, he wept aloud.[1]

He was later picked by Mission Board President Elias Cornelius to attend Cornwall. Buck traveled with the prominent missionary through Washington, D.C., where he met Secretary of War John Calhoun and President James Monroe.

He also met the founder of the American Bible Society and current mission board member Elias Boudinot, who had served at one time as the chairman of the Continental

Congress. Boudinot believed in the Indian cause to the degree that he had written a book arguing that the Native Americans were actually the lost ten tribes of Israel. He took a special interest in the promising and impressionable young Cherokee.

The celebrated statesman asked the young man if he would like to take his name, a practice not uncommon in the day.

Buck Watie accepted the flattering offer. He was known for the rest of his life as Elias Boudinot.*

He was called Boudinot at Cornwall, but the prestigious Caucasian name was no help to him in the current crisis with Harriet. Added to that pain for Buck—the more conscientious of the two cousins—was his concern regarding the trouble this alliance may bring to his people. It could permanently damage relationships with prominent men in Washington like his namesake Mr. Boudinot or other members of the mission board who were fighting for the rights of the Cherokees against the likes of Andrew Jackson.

The protests against his proposed marriage now brought to the surface just how complex and confused was this rela-

*Pronounced "Boo-din-ote" or "Boo-din-ott"—with a hard 'T'—by most descendents and historians.

tionship between the missionaries and the Cherokees. The two had never quite connected.

At the time of Washington's treaty three decades earlier, Secretary of War Henry Knox called for missionaries to help the Indians acculturate—to teach the arts of literacy, husbandry, farming, and other facets of civilized life.

After the Gambolds arrived in 1801, the first high-profile missionary, Presbyterian Gideon Blackburn, met with Cherokee chiefs in 1803 with the offer to build schools. He had served as a chaplain in the opposing frontier armies "with a bible in one hand and a rifle in the other." With his long mane of white hair and tremendous enthusiasm, Blackburn had in a short time educated hundreds of Cherokee students at mission schools in Sale Creek and Tellico and raised a substantial amount of money toward the project.

Blackburn had all the zeal for evangelism expected of a missionary. He believed in the Cherokees' spiritual equality, proclaiming them "of the same [human] race with ourselves. . . . As soon as they are civilized, their way will be open for the establishment of regular religious society."

But cultural equality was another story. Progress meant seeing Cherokee culture give way to European ways. Children were immediately given English names chosen by Blackburn. The missionary's wife taught them to prepare "victuals in American style." As quickly as possible, the half-naked Indian children were neatly clothed in stripped cotton or plain linen, manufactured in Tennessee.[2]

Immediately condemned were ancient cultural practices such as polygamy and abortion, which was applied after the third child to prevent encumbrances related to war and hunting. By 1819, the missionaries had convinced the chiefs to pass a law forbidding a white man to take more than one wife. But for Cherokee men, the council said one wife was simply "recommended."[3]

The council was also convinced to pass laws discouraging gambling, card playing, dice throwing and attending the theatre. Billiard parlors had to be licensed.

Much more controversial was the missionaries' strong stand against "conjuring," a practice of medical healing and spiritual and economic problem-solving involving herbs and real-world activity along with spiritual prayers.

Dances were employed to end a drought. Or, to increase the chances of winning at a ballplay, an athlete might avoid eating rabbit, whose bones were weak, or bottom-dwelling fish who were sluggish. Players prayed to the deer to be swift, the rattlesnake to be fierce, the red bat to be elusive, and the hawk for piercing vision.

One old conjurer told missionary Daniel Butrick that thunder came from a cave in Raccoon Mountain. In explaining the mysteries of healing, he said, "when they call on eagles, butterflies, etc. to help them perform cures, they do not mean eagles as we see but beings above who we give the same names."

On one occasion, missionary William Chamberlain was able to distinguish between the two sides of conjuring. He told a woman that "it was very good for her to administer medicine to the sick, but it was not good to use the art of conjuring."

But mostly the missionaries found it impossible to distinguish between the two. Daniel Butrick tells of a ninety-year-old woman who traveled twenty miles to be baptized. She appeared "sincerely converted in every respect excepting she expressed unwillingness to renounce conjuring. She had for years been a conjuress." Notwithstanding the deep passion the missionaries held for conversion and adding to their numbers, they reported that nearly half of one congregation had been suspended for returning to their old religion. "One of them said he thought the service of Satan as sweet as the service of God," wrote an alarmed Chamberlain.[4]

One zealous Cherokee convert burned down the town council house in Etowah. He called it "the Devil's meeting house" because the meetings were opened with old rituals and dances. Traditionalists reacted with threats to burn down the mission houses.[5]

Historian Marion Starkey, who presents the missionaries in a positive light despite identifying several shortcomings, notes that some flexibility was allowed regarding polygamy. A convert with multiple wives was allowed to remain married to all of them. "Butrick ransacked his New Testament" to see what the apostles had done regarding polygamy, writes Starkey. "So far as he could see they had done nothing.

"A similar tolerance to other Cherokee ways might have borne fruit; for instance, a more sympathetic attitude toward such Cherokee rites as the various dances, Green, Corn, Bear, Eagle, the ceremony of Going to the Water, ball plays, the New Fire. The missionaries objected to all of these because they involved conjure.

"The spirit of some of the ceremonies, however, was not unlike the spirit of many a Christian ceremony. The Green Corn Festival had some kinship with the Pilgrim Thanksgiving. Going to the Water, except for the conjure man's abracadabra with beads, resembled baptism." The New Fire resembled Easter. "All pious hearths were extinguished on a day in March and rekindled from a torch lit at the 'new fire' kindled by the medicine men."

Likewise, the ballplays were noble efforts with exacting ethical standards worthy of a more sympathetic study by the missionaries. "The most respectable men of the community were given supervision of the local ball play to make sure it was honestly conducted. . . . The conjure involved in preparing for a game was of the disciplinary sort—going to the river . . . avoiding women . . . all-night vigils, and strenuous preparatory dances. . . . It was indeed nearly as rousing, as male, as dangerous, as the warpath. It had been formerly allied with the rites of the warpath and still remained for the Cherokees a moral equivalent of war. They did not propose to let white men take it away from them."[6]

It was true that the prevalence of the white man's whiskey at ballplays had greatly multiplied any aspect of brawling or sexual activity that may have existed before, but the council refused to outlaw ballplays despite the strong condemnations. The Cherokees "still retain their grossest vices," wrote Rev. Isaac Proctor. "Those that are most heathenish are their Ball Plays, where the players are literally naked and yet a large proportion of the spectators are females. The all-night dances are attended by wives without their husbands and husbands without their wives, and as they are held during the night, we may safely infer that all the deeds of darkness are committed."[7]

The relationship between the Cherokees and the missionaries grew more difficult after Rev. Blackburn suddenly ended his initiatives in 1810 under a cloud of secrecy and suspicion. According to Tennessee Governor John Sevier's journal, the missionary had some side activities in progress: a group of Creek Indians intercepted two fully loaded flatboats on the Tennessee river several miles below Chattanooga. They "seized upon and took Parson Blackburn's whiskey."

Blackburn was in fact a distiller of liquor, a practice not frowned upon for clergy in the early 1800s. But selling liquor to Indians was against the law. Those who knew but little of the scandal may have concluded that Blackburn left for that legal violation. However, careful research over a century later shows that Blackburn, always a patriot, had agreed to help the federal government in a secret mission to identify a waterway through Indian territory that could reach to the gulf—all in the name of protecting the frontier and under the auspices of transporting whiskey.[8]

The few chiefs who understood the real reason for Blackburn's extracurricular activity kept the matter silent enough for missionary activity to continue. But nevertheless, added strain on the relationship was inevitable.

Blackburn's focus on converting Cherokee individuals but not Cherokee culture was most evident in language.

He concluded that the children had no need for the Cherokee tongue, and he stepped up efforts for teaching English. The instructors did not learn the language but rather left the translating to bilingual students of mixed race.

Rev. Gambold agreed with Blackburn that it was useless to try to learn the "wretched Cherokee language." There were so many dialects that, to Gambold, it sounded like several different languages.

"Some of the words and syllables are pronounced through one's nose, some get stuck in one's throat; frequently it is sufficient to have the tongue touch the gums or the lips lightly. Their tones are often such that no possible combination of our vowels can produce the desired sound."

Blackburn's departure left a void in the Cherokee Nation that the American Mission Board was anxious to fill. It took almost a decade until the Brainerd Mission was established. And those missionaries were now identified with the sentiments of their predecessors like Gambold. "The study of their language would in a great measure prove but time and labor lost," he said. "It seems desirable that their language, customs, manner of thinking, etc, should be forgotten." Gambold's great object was "to rescue the aboriginal man himself from the destruction which awaits his race, rather than [to rescue] his history, language, customs, etc."[9]

The missionaries at Brainerd also found great difficulty in learning and translating the language. They resorted to bilingual students for translation. Historian Starkey points to their classical training: "Anyone who had been exposed to Boston believed that mastery of a language entailed the memorization of paradigms and rules of grammar. Cherokee had never been broken to such a harness; its syntactical variety was infinite and elusive."[10]

In fact, the American Mission Board had commissioned the eminent philologist William Pickering to devise a system of transliteration suitable for all Native American languages. But the efforts continued to bear little fruit. Consequently, full-blooded Cherokees tended to struggle at the schools. Missionary Hoyt noted that Cherokees were anxious to be educated, but "especially the half-breeds." Another missionary reported that the school was made up of "children of half and a quarter Cherokee and the children of white men with native wives."

The full-blooded children were very slow to learn English. Even a small portion of white blood seemed to help certain students gain an inclination toward the European language, as was the case with John and Buck.

They were both considered full-bloods, but in fact had one white great-grandfather whose name is lost to history.

The emergence of two classes of Cherokees became a concern for the missionaries. "There is a very great difference between the highest and lowest class," wrote Butrick. "Unless peculiar caution is used, two parties will be formed which will probably be called, though falsely, the Christian and Pagan party."

Rev. Isaac Proctor urged more preaching to bring the "degraded, dull Cherokees to a level with the half Cherokees."[11]

Andrew Jackson was always quick to exploit the two-class phenomenon. Whenever the Cherokees resisted his efforts of removal, he insisted the majority of the nation, the full-bloods, wanted to go westward toward the forests, while the minority of mixed-bloods resisted out of self-interest in their growing properties.

"The real Indians, the natives of the forest, are little concerned" about removal, he told John Calhoun. The problem was with "designing half-breeds and renegade white men."[12]

Into this crisis entered a new missionary from New England, the Rev. Samuel A. Worcester, whose enthusiasm for the Cherokee language and whose linguistic capabilities raised the hopes of leaders in Brainerd and New England that progress could be made.

Worcester had heard about the rumors of a new alphabet developed by the reclusive silversmith George Gist who spoke no English. Scholars in New England were skeptical, but the twenty-eight-year-old Worcester—who came from a line of eight generations of Congregational ministers and whose father presided over Vermont College—believed in the unbelievable reports.

The first pages of Worcester's journal exhibit his tremendous enthusiasm and inclination toward the kind of detail needed to master a language. On Novmber 5, 1825, he quickly scaled the heights of Lookout Mountain. There he discovered a waterfall and a series of caves to which he devotes three pages of description in his journal along with detailed drawings and charts.

Rain hindered him from returning to Brainerd, so he "spent the afternoon in attention to Guyst's (Gist's) alphabet." The next day, also rainy, was spent "transcribing Cherokee hymns into Guyst's alphabet."

The other missionaries had apparently renewed their hopes that perhaps someone could unravel the Cherokee language, which was considered as difficult as Chinese.

"They rejoice that my instructions are to acquire the Cherokee language," he wrote a few days later. "They unite in saying that to apply myself assiduously to the language, and to make other things bend to that object, is the best way to employ my time."[13]

His early journal entries mention that Butrick preached from Romans 12 on being a living sacrifice for God and also about the final judgment. The first two sermons preached by Worcester were from Thessalonians 5: "Rejoice always, pray without ceasing, " and from 1 Corinthians 13: 1–7, the famous chapter on love—a passage, according to his journal, he preached often. The opening line had direct application to his current obsession with language: "If I speak in the tongues of men and angels, but have not love, I am nothing." The text he chose most often, according to his journal, was the same used by missionary Cornelius in that first sermon at Brainerd: "What does if profit a man if he gains the whole world, yet loses his own soul?"

As important to Worcester as learning the language was the nation's ability to print and distribute the language. So his other obsession was acquiring a printing press, the most advanced and powerful communications medium of the age. In a council as early as 1822, the chiefs passed a resolution to obtain a printing press, but the precise mechanical devices were difficult to obtain and they were expensive. In fact, Elias Boudinot had been charged to raise money for the effort during his speaking tours.

Worcester had already identified Boudinot, also a gifted linguist (he read Virgil and the Greek philosophers in their original languages[14]) as perhaps the very person who could help the nation conquer the language barrier.

Worcester also had another, more controversial plan. He knew that a newspaper published in both Cherokee and English might be just the tool to awaken the United States citizens toward the Cherokee cause. And Boudinot would make the perfect editor.

However, Buck had other more heart-wrenching matters to consider. The brewing crisis in Cornwall had the potential to render him useless for the cause.

CHAPTER SEVEN

THE RIOT

The prominent members of Harriet Gold's family now asked on a frequent basis about the health of Colonel Benjamin Gold's youngest daughter. They heard she hovered between life and death.

The cause of the illness had been kept secret from Harriet's thirteen siblings, including from sister Mary and her husband General D. B. Brinsmead, from sister Flora who was married to Cornwall instructor Herman Vaill, and from her brother Stephen Gold, who was her closest family member and particularly devoted to her. "What one knew, the other knew."

The patient was locked up in the sick room of the home with visits only from Dr. Gold, the nephew of Harriet's father.

"Our parents thought it best not to tell the rest of the family," wrote Mary. "Harriet was in a delicate state of health—and they thought she could not bear it."

But, eventually, the parents grew concerned that their own beliefs may send their daughter to her grave. "Our parents felt . . . that they might be found fighting against

God—and some time during Harriet's sickness they told her they should oppose her no longer. She must do what she thought best."

Harriet revived immediately. Her first order of business was to break the news to her brother, Stephen. Cousin Ellen Gibbs reports that she chose to write him a letter.

"One evening they were as usual together in the parlor conversing when she handed him the letter; there were two doors; one she locked before they went in, she went out and locked the other, and gave the key to her mother, telling her not to let him out until he became quiet.

"He screamed and called Harriet, Harriet like a madman. She locked herself in her room upstairs and would not come out until he promised he would behave. That was before it was publicly known."[1]

Stephen, however, wasted no time informing his in-laws Herman Vaill and General Brinsmead. "The dye is cast. Harriet is gone," he wrote them. "Words cannot, no—let imagination only express, the feelings of my heart."[2]

Brinsmead, a trustee at the Cornwall Mission School, immediately informed his fellow trustees, who became "as white as sheets." Rev. Timothy Stone protested, calling it a lie. But after hearing Brinsmead out, "his mouth was stopped."

Another pastor, Rev. Joseph Harvey, then rode to the Gold home to confront the parents, demanding to know if they had consented to the mixed union. They told him the matter lay entirely in Harriet's hands. Then he confronted Harriet.

"The following Sunday, Rev. Harvey preached at Cornwall," writes Boudinot biographer Ralph Gabriel. "No doubt his glance rose from that peaceful and unsuspecting congregation to Harriet sitting in the choir as he thought of the secret which she harbored." Later, he handed her a letter. "It was an ultimatum to be answered within three days. The reply would immediately be submitted to a special meeting of the Board of Agents. If Harriet should give up her Indian, the agents would enjoin secrecy and the affair would never be known. If she refused, they would publish banns [a public announcement regarding the marriage] in the manner which seemed to them most fitting."

When Harriet replied that she planned to be a missionary and marry Buck, Connecticut's most famous preacher, Lyman Beecher, rode his horse to Cornwall and led a meeting at which the agents prepared a special report regarding Harriet Gold and Elias Boudinot which was published on June 17:

"We, the undersigned, being a part of the Agency of the Foreign Mission School…have recently become acquainted with the fact that a negotiation for a marriage has been carried on secretly between Elias Boudinot, a young Cherokee, who left the school with good character and Harriet R. Gold of this village; and that this negotiation which has been carried on by secret and covered correspondence, has now become a settled engagement between the parties.

"We regard those who have engaged in or accessory to this transaction, as criminal; as offering insult to the known feelings of the Christian community; and as sporting with the sacred interests of this charitable institution. . . . Let the blame fall where it justly belongs."

Cornwall erupted at the news. Harriet was swifted away and hidden in another house that overlooked the village green. From that vantage point she could see a crowd of "respectable young ladies and gentlemen" who let their anger turn into mob behavior. The key characters were burned in effigy.

"A painting had before been prepared representing a beautiful young lady and an Indian, [along with] a woman as an instigator of Indian marriages," wrote Harriet. "Brother Stephen set fire to the barrel of tar—or rather funeral pile. The flames rose high, and the smoke ascended—some said it reminded them of the smoke of their torment which they feared would ascend forever. My heart truly sang with anguish at the dreadful scene."

Gibbs reports that Harriet looked out and said, "Father, forgive them; they know not what they do."

The irony was not lost on Harriet. "Even the most unprincipled say they never heard anything so bad even among the heathen as that of burning a sister in effigy."

She said the crowd planned another meeting for the next evening. "I have seen the time when I could close my eyes upon every earthly object and look up to God as my only supporter, my only hope—when I could with emotion I never felt before say to my heavenly Father, 'Other refuge have I none, so I helpless hang on thee.'"

The following Sunday, the wife of Rev. Timothy Stone instructed the young ladies of the choir, of which Harriet was previously a member, to wear black crepe paper on their left arm.

None of these activities, however cruel or outrageous, changed Harriet's mind. And so her family members decided to appeal to her more righteous instincts. They accused her of threatening the extinction of the mission school and said if she continued in her decision she would be harming the cause of Christ.

General Brinsmead commissioned brother-in-law Herman Vaill with the duty. "Our parents have long since given their written consent to the union through Harriet's craftiness by making them believe she should die if she did not have her Indian last winter," the general wrote. "The whole family are to be sacrificed to gratify, if I may so express, the animal feelings of one of its number. And lo! The whole is clothed in the garb of religion—'they could not fight against God' is the reply."

So Vaill composed a letter of 5,000 words to Harriet.

"There is a wide difference between going [to the mission field] because we love the cause of Christ . . . and going because we love another object, and have a selfish inducement," he told Harriet.

Vaill conceded that mixed marriages weren't necessarily sinful. And he admitted he had no objection to Boudinot, whom he knew personally. But the purpose of the mission school was to make the heathen obedient subjects to the kingdom of Christ. If the mission school closed, it would injure the interests of missions. "Less of a missionary spirit will prevail, fewer missionary sermons will be preached. Less money will be contributed," he warned, "and more of the heathen will be lost."

The end of his letter aimed for the soul, saying Harriet's actions gave the enemy occasion to blaspheme God. "You will bring dishonour upon the Saviour," he charged. "You will by the same stroke open his wounds afresh. You profess to be his disciple. He expects his disciples engaged supremely in the interests of his Kingdom. For this Kingdom he has bled; and O Harriet, He has already bled enough.

"Do not go away like Cain and Judas, but come back like Peter. Will you go? If you are a hypocrite, and designed for a reprobate, doubtless you will. But if you are a Christian, it must be you will listen, and regard the advice of friends, and the call of God and his church. As ever, your affectionate brother, H.L. Vaill."

In the Cherokee Nation, Elias Boudinot was left to consider how he must act in response to the public outrage and the turmoil he was causing for the Gold family. He was not as quick as his cousin John to defy all adversaries. And he now had many questions about how his Cherokee culture related to his Christian faith.

The next report was not a good one in the view of the Christian community. Elias Boudinot was spotted attending a heathen ballplay. To make matters worse, the ballplay was on a Sabbath.

Missionary Moody Hall called it a "scene of national iniquity." He expected "better things" of Boudinot. The missionaries spread reports throughout the region of the "fallen young man."[3]

American Board for Foreign Missions (Jeremiah Evarts second from left)

CHAPTER EIGHT

THE TRUCE

Thousands of settlers continued to pour in from Europe. They migrated south from Philadelphia and Baltimore down the great wagon trail through Virginia into Tennessee. Others moved northward from the heart of Georgia. They continually pressed into the Cherokee borders.

"The soil is fertile beyond description" and the Indians are wasting it, wrote citizens from Tennessee and Georgia to the President. The Cherokee land is "propitious to the culture of cotton" and has great "commercial advantage." Not only that, "the Hero who has since immortalized Himself" had won the land for them in the War of 1812.

The state of Georgia, alarmed by the Cherokees' growing political self-awareness, printed a resolution circulated far and wide demanding the immediate and total extinction of all Cherokee title to land within its borders. And now the federal government planned to stop protecting the Cherokee borders, a clause in the treaty with Washington that the United States agreed to as part of their concern that the Cherokees not take up arms again.

Jackson agreed wholeheartedly with Georgia's claims. "It is high time to do away with the farce of treating with Indian tribes as sovereign nations," he said, calling the whole concept "an absurdity in politics."

Federal agent R. J. Meigs lamented that the treaty used the words "solemn guarantee" instead of "allotted." The Cherokees now believed they could build an empire within an empire and had "erroneous ideas of their sovereignty and independence." He called the whole notion "a monster in politics."

Unlike Jackson, Meigs still left some room for including the Cherokees' consent. He would not "deprive them of their natural right—my mind would revolve at such a sentiment." But, ultimately, "they were, at the close of the Revolution, a conquered people. . . . Their lands were forfeited," and "they were considered as minors."

As minors, they were entitled to treaty protection, he said, and they could be forced to agree to treaties. If they pushed for sovereignty, they could no longer expect to be protected. This "would soon seal their destruction."[1]

The Cherokees had laid down their weapons in 1794, staking all their hopes on the binding legal promises provided in the federal treaty. President Washington was relieved to see the frontier's most notorious warring tribe consent to a lawful peace after a long history of strife between whites and natives in the New World.

From 1607 to 1622 a tolerable peace existed between the two peoples. Although they did not acknowledge the Indians' title to the lands, "the English still tried always to purchase such land before taking it over, thus to respect Indian dignity and natural law," wrote historian Roy Harvey Pearce.

But that deference to natural law ended on April 1, 1622, when suddenly, without warning, the Indians attacked a hundred-mile area and killed at least 347 settlers. The Indians no longer had any rights. Europeans "may now by a right of Warre, and law of Nations, invade the Country, and destroy them that sought to destroy us."

When the Puritans arrived in New England to establish the new Israel and a biblical "City on a Hill," they exchanged natural law arguments for divine law.

They argued that the natives had failed miserably in obeying the first commandment in Genesis to cultivate and till the earth. The agrarian English were obliged to take it over.

In a world where everything had a biblical metaphor, the Indians became potential converts as well as the symbol for the enemies of God—"a man who had to be brought to the civilized responsibilities of Christian manhood," wrote Pearce, "a wild man to be improved along with wild lands, a creature who had to be made into a Puritan if he was to be saved. Save him, and you saved one of Satan's victims. Destroy him, and you destroyed one of Satan's partisans."

After the massacre of the Pequots, the Rev. Solomon Stoddard explained that the Indians were like the Philistines. "Should not Christians have more mercy and compassion? But I would refer you to David's war. We had sufficient light from the word of God for our proceedings."

Nevertheless, he called for compassion on the "Brutish Persons. . . . It is an act of love to our own nature to seek their salvation."

Rhode Island founder Roger Williams also worked to convert Indians with their "hideous worship of creatures and devils," as did Puritan leader Cotton Mather who called them "the veriest ruins of mankind."

Despite the Puritan missionary zeal, little fruit emerged from their efforts. And when New England threw off much of its religious heritage, it continued to find itself with contradictory views on the Native Americans.

Enlightened thinkers now came to admire certain Indian foods and practices such as the "wondrous custom" of offering maidens of the village to distinguished visitors.

They believed Indians had lost their innocence due to drunkenness and luxury brought by the British. They were happy in their simple "State of Nature" and could only lament the arrival of the Europeans.

North Carolina's John Lawson wrote about the essential integrity of the savage life, an integrity destroyed by civilization. Virginia's William Byrd II spoke of Indian people as warring, cunning, and malicious, yet "contented with Nature as they find her."

The savage now became understood "as someone who had not and somehow could not progress into the civilized, who would inevitably be destroyed by the civilized, the lesser good necessarily giving way to the greater," as Pearce put it. "Americans were thus of two minds about the Indian whom they were destroying. They pitied his state but saw it as inevitable; they hoped to bring him to civilization but saw that civilization would destroy him."

The sentiment by 1779 was neatly summed up when frontier general John Sullivan offered a toast on the Fourth of July: "Civilization or death to all American Savages."[2]

Those "savages" had further complicated the lives of frontiersmen like Sullivan during the French and Indian War and, later, the revolutionary conflict. The British viewed the Indians in the same category as the colonists: subjects but citizens. However, the colonists, particularly those in the Southern states, viewed the Indians at a level close to slavery.

In 1763, the British sent two Indian agents into the western frontier to encourage trade and to enforce the boundary line at the Appalachian Mountains drawn to keep settlers away from Indian territory.

The agent sent south was John McDonald, a Scotsman from Inverness who married a half-blood Cherokee at Fort Loudon in Tennessee. Her father, William Shorey, had mastered the language and so did McDonald—a rare feat.

McDonald set up his trading post and farm 100 miles south of Fort Loudon on Chickamauga Creek (the spot he would later sell to the Brainerd Mission). He was the first European to settle in the area, and his daughter married the son of another early settler, Daniel Ross. Ross's son was John Ross, McDonald's grandson.

When hostilities broke out between England and America, it was natural for the Cherokee-speaking McDonald to encourage an alliance with the British. The Upper Cherokees remained neutral. But the other half of the nation, led by Dragging Canoe, moved southward and set up headquarters at McDonald's trading post on Chickamauga Creek. The fierce Cherokee warriors were dubbed "Chickamaugas."[3]

One of those warriors was the Ridge. He joined at the age of seventeen when the war with England was over and President Washington was working desperately to establish peace on the frontier. Both Washington and his Secretary of War, Henry Knox, who oversaw Indian relations, worried about the abuse of natural and legal rights toward the Indians.

In its treaties the federal government "solemnly guaranteed" the lands held by the tribes. In a speech to Congress, Knox angered the frontiersman with his declaration: "The Indians, being prior occupants, possess the right to the soil. It cannot be taken away from them unless by their free consent. To dispossess them in any other principle would be a gross violation of the fundamental laws of nature and of that distributive justice which is the glory of a nation."[4]

But Dragging Canoe was convinced, and rightly so, that Knox did not represent the sentiment of most of the southern people as well as many in the North. Though the upper chiefs, led by Hanging Maw, had signed the 1785 Treaty of Hopewell, the muscular and pockmarked Dragging Canoe warned that this agreement would be broken as well. The Real People, he said, would be forced to seek refuge in some distant wilderness.[5]

Three young warriors, the Ridge, White Path, and Doublehead, led the nation into civilization over the next several decades. But even after Dragging Canoe's death in 1792, these young warriors continued to fight bloody battles, thanks in part to the assassination of Hanging Maw by renegade frontiersmen.

Finally, after a Tennessee regiment destroyed the Chickamauga headquarters at McDonald's trading post, the Cherokee holdouts surrendered and finalized Washington's Treaty in 1794. But not before the Ridge watched Doublehead lead an attack at Cavett's Station next to Fort Loudon (near Knoxville, Tennessee). As the thirteen settlers, mostly women and children, came out of the fort waving a white flag, Doublehead and his men ignored the surrender and massacred all but one of the Unakas—a five-year-old boy snatched away by Ridge and a colleague before the tomahawk of the bloodthirsty warriors split his head open.

The Ridge rushed into the forest and wept. It was the the turning point of his life from "savage" to statesman.[6]

With the later exception of the execution of Doublehead, considered a lawful and necessary act by the rest of the chiefs, the Ridge had argued for nonviolent peace and the rule of law for the Cherokee Nation. He and the other chiefs also rejected Tecumseh's strategy of taking up arms for survival.

But with the strength of the federal treaties now weakened by the states, the Cherokees knew that their most crucial ally had become the federal government's chief executive. Their fate lay in the President's interpretation of the treaty and his willingness to enforce the document.

Route of Western Removal

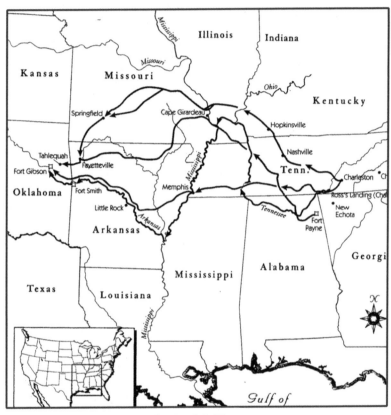

*From Michael Bergan, *The Trail Of Tears.*

CHAPTER NINE
THE INVENTION

I n 1824, the Cherokee Nation sent a delegation to President James Monroe. The Ridge led the group that included John Ross, George Lowry, and Elijah Hicks, with John Ridge interpreting.

Secretary of State John Quincy Adams noted that Major Ridge addressed the President "in the figurative style of savage oratory, with frequent recurrence to the idea of the Great Spirit above."

During the federal agents' most recent entreaty for land cessions and removal, the chiefs asked them why they did not understand their resolve: "The Cherokee Nation have now come to a decisive and unalterable conclusion not to cede away any more land," the chiefs reminded them. To demonstrate their independence, the nation then voted to send their delegation straight to Washington without permission and without an invitation. An incensed federal agent conceded their "consistency" but said they should be taught "better manners."[1]

The Ridge and Ross and the rest of the delegation asked President Monroe and Adams—both more neutral federalists—and the less sympathetic John C. Calhoun, Secretary of War, to intercede with Congress to correct Georgia's demands for the extinguishment of their lands.

Calhoun told them firmly that it was impossible for them to remain as a distinct society in the states. "Such a community is incompatible with our system," he said, noting the clause in the Constitution forbidding the creation of states within another state.

The Cherokee delegation was equally firm. "Sir, we beg leave to remind you that the Cherokees are not foreigners but original inhabitants of the United States," they said. The Cherokees "cannot recognize the sovereignty of any state within the limits of their territory."

Reports of the delegation's impressive arguments caused outrage in the Georgia legislature. They were especially angry to hear that Calhoun greeted them as "gentlemen," suspecting some deep design in his word choice.

"These misguided men," they wrote to the President, "should be taught by the general government that there is no alternative between their removal beyond the limits of the state of Georgia and their extinction."

The President considered the letter from Georgia an insult. Adams called it "a most acrimonious reproach against the United States." He was the one most impressed with the Cherokees. "They write their own state papers, and reason as logically as most white diplomats." (The Georgians had accused them of using ghost writers.)

The chiefs could also be entertaining. Major Ridge's "fine figure and handsome face" made a great impression during a dinner party at the home of Calhoun. Chief George Lowry found himself at the dinner table with a Georgia congressman who on the floor of the House referred to Cherokees as "savages subsisting upon roots, wild herbs and disgusting reptiles." So Lowry pointed to a dish of sweet potatoes and loudly requested the waiter to bring him "some of those roots." He caught everyone's attention and gained a round of laughter each time he took only a small portion and kept requesting more potatoes. "We Indians are very fond of roots," he said.

The delegation also demanded that the United States honor an 1804 treaty that guaranteed to the nation a payment of an additional $1,000 a year, a sum they had never received. Calhoun at first denied the existence of such a treaty, but the chiefs showed him the signed original. Clerks combed the War Department archives and found their long lost copy. Calhoun agreed to its terms.

When President Monroe later gave his annual message to Congress, he made an announcement that angered the

Georgians: "There is no obligation on the United States to remove the Indians by force."

But that statement was quickly qualified with another that revealed Monroe's own personal opinion that removal was in the Cherokees' best interest: "All these evils may be avoided," he said, "if these tribes *will consent* to remove beyond the limits of our present states and territories."[2]

The President's equivocation revealed the political danger of his position, and the fact that public opinion one way or the other could affect Monroe's resolve. With the highly popular Jackson building momentum with his position on the Indian Question, the fate of the Cherokees had moved into a public relations war.

Popular sentiment was further endangered by the Cherokees' involvement with other nations, especially the Creeks, in showing them the way toward political independence.

John Ridge, now an accomplished lawyer, was asked to join the Creeks in their delegation to Washington and actually wrote their legal protests against Georgia's demand for land cessions.

The Creeks voted to "follow the pattern of the Cherokees." And their resolves echoed the Cherokee councils. "On no account whatever will we consent to sell one more foot of land." Like Tecumseh before them, the Cherokees were attempting to form a new alliance of tribes. But this war was not a military battle. It was a legal strategy.

Federal agents complained of "a steady and officious interference" in Creek affairs by the Cherokees. John Ridge was called "a dangerous, meddling man."[3]

The argument that the "real" full-bloods wanted removal gained support in the public. "[The Cherokee] government is an aristocracy consisting of about 100 men called Chiefs, and those Chiefs are controlled by perhaps twenty speculating individuals," wrote one agent. And Jackson was always quick to denounce scheming half-breeds.[4]

Missionary Samuel Worcester was keen enough to see that the larger Cherokee population needed to advance in literacy if the support of the public—and thus the support of the President—was to remain strong for the Cherokees and their treaty rights.

Worcester believed the answer lie in the newly developed alphabet of George Gist, known later in life by his Cherokee name, Sequoyah. Worcester observed numbers of full-blood Cherokees picking up Sequoyah's system in a matter of days, and the missionary quickly sent up to

Boston instructions for casting type in Sequoyan for the printing press.

But the Board in New England rejected Sequoyah's system, which was not actually an alphabet but a syllabary. The eccentric silversmith conquered the complex tongue by identifying seventy-six syllables instead of an alphabet of consonants and vowels. It took the Cherokees a bit longer to memorize than an alphabet, but once all the possible syllables were mastered, a people who had never used the talking book found themselves reading and writing within a few days.

However, the Boston divines believed Worcester had fallen for an unfounded wind of enthusiasm. Seventy-six characters were too many, too complex. They wrote back and said Pickering's system of writing should be used instead.

Butrick tried to convince the chiefs to agree to Pickering's system or else the Board would get "discouraged." But Worcester refused to give up, writing to the board on how the chiefs had rejected Pickering's system and were already circulating hymns and letters in Sequoyan.

"Tell them now of printing in another character and you throw water upon the fire," he said. "In the meantime, a crisis in the nation is passing by, and when at such crisis such an enthusiasm is kindled, it must be cherished, not repressed, if you would save the nation."[5]

Sequoyah initially spent years making marks on sticks of bark with pokeberry juice. John Ridge pointed out that the years of effort before Sequoyah's success were very difficult for the man who hobbled on a shrunken leg from a hunting accident. He always wore the traditional Cherokee turban and smoked incessantly from a long-stemmed pipe. He was even accused of witchcraft: "His corn was left to weeds and he was pronounced a crazy man by the tribe," said Ridge. "His wife thought so too, and burned up his manuscripts whenever she could find them. But he persevered."

The silversmith's original strategy was to engrave a distinct figure for every word of the complex language, like the Chinese method. Then he discovered the seventy-six syllables. "Having accomplished this, he called together six of his neighbors and said, 'Now, I can make a book.' But they did not believe him."

He then sent his little daughter over to the chiefs with a message that provided enough evidence for them to commission an official test. A group of young men with sharp minds were sent to Sequoyah's cabin with a message. They returned and, in front of the chiefs, handed the document from Sequoyah to another group of young men, instructed in the syllabary. The exact message was read back to the chiefs from the "talking leaf." Sequoyah became a tribal hero, and a feast was held in his honor.

Until then, only ten percent of the Cherokees had learned to read and write in English. But within a few years of Sequoyah's discovery, two-thirds of the nation became literate in the new Cherokee script. Even Boston's John Pickering was convinced: "Both children and grown persons actually acquire the art of reading in the course of a few days!" A former Secretary of the Treasury, Albert Gallatin, marveled at the independently created system and instantly learned language, a phenomenon that stands unique in history: "The boy learns in a few weeks that which occupied two years of the time of our boys," he said.[6]

These reports and the perseverance of Worcester convinced the Board members in Boston to cast the type for the printing press in Sequoyan. Worcester had immediate plans to translate and publish Bibles and hymnbooks as soon as possible. But he was also focused on the more ambitious plan: a Cherokee newspaper.

For these projects he needed both a translator and an editor—someone of enormous intellect and talent. He was convinced that the man he had in mind, Elias Boudinot, could recover from his scandal.

Five days before Christmas, Worcester invited Boudinot to his home, and they spent the evening talking together. The missionary then fired off a letter to Boston with a positive report on the supposedly fallen young man.

"I have more confidence in Boudinot as a translator than in any other," he later wrote. "And, though I may be deceived, and some have greatly doubted, [I have] quite a respect for his character."[7]

Rev. Samuel Worcester

Sequoyah

CHAPTER TEN
THE CONSTITUTION

Soon after his reconciliation with Worcester and the missionaries, Buck regained the courage to consider traveling back to Cornwall. There he would face his detractors and, God willing, marry his beloved Harriet.

Meanwhile, he and his mentor worked tirelessly on translation. The trick with Cherokee was the very complicated verb. Boudinot identified 178 forms of the phrase "to tie." And that was only in the present tense indicative mood—there were twenty-nine other moods. He declared the Cherokee verb the most complicated in the world.

Worcester agreed. "A single word in Cherokee requires often several English words to translate it," he said. English pronouns, adverbs, and prepositions might all be found in the variations of the Cherokee verb.

While Worcester praised Boudinot for his linguistic genius, Buck had similar admiration: "Mr. Worcester proceeds rapidly in acquiring the language. He intends to preach in it. The blessings of God attend him."[1]

Worcester continued his preaching to a number of missions in the nation, often riding up to forty or fifty miles a day, sometimes sleeping in the woods. His journal records Matthew 16:26 as a favorite sermon passage: "What shall it profit a man if he gains the whole world, yet loses his own soul?"

Buck agreed to Worcester's offer to become editor of the newspaper, but only on the condition that Worcester move to New Echota, the new Cherokee capital city sixty miles south near Calhoun, Georgia. He said the flood-prone Brainerd was too damp and affected his health. Worcester consented.

New Echota meant "New Town," and it referenced the ancient town of Chota that served as a city of refuge for Cherokees who would otherwise be killed by clan members of someone who had died in an accident—ancient laws had no allowance for manslaughter. The new town of refuge had its streets laid out and buildings constructed specifically for governing, not unlike Washington, D.C. Although the two-story council house was humbler than the domed Capitol building, the Cherokees were very proud of it.

There were several other structures, including a Supreme Court building and one for the printing press and offices of the *Cherokee Phoenix*, the name given to the new

Cherokee paper. Articles, announcements, advertisements, stories from abroad, and laws relevant to the
Cherokee plight were printed in Sequoyan on one side
and English on the other. A large number of older
Cherokees purchased spectacles to better read the exciting
new publication.[2]

Boudinot subscribed to 100 different newspapers in
order to keep up with current affairs. The *Phoenix* itself was
widely read and mailed throughout the country.

One of the first items in the newspaper was the draft of
the Cherokee Constitution now being considered by the
council. It reflected the U.S.'s sacred document, with three
branches of government and checks and balances placed
on each branch. And it was even bolder with its Christian
language:

"We, the Representatives of the People of the Cherokee
Nation, in Convention assembled, in order to establish justice, ensure tranquility, promote our common welfare, and
secure to ourselves and to our posterity the blessing of liberty; acknowledging with humility and gratitude the good-
ness of the Sovereign Ruler of the Universe . . . do ordain
and establish this Constitution for the Government of the
Cherokee Nation."

The document differed from the U.S. in its declaration
of communally owned land by the nation and in its

requirement that all elected officials must publicly state belief in God. However, it mirrored the U.S. Constitution in forbidding Blacks to vote—many chiefs had plantations now and were slave owners, including John Ross and the Ridges.[3]

When Elias Boudinot finally mustered the courage to travel back to Connecticut, he decided to wear a disguise when he reached the outskirts of Cornwall in case a lynching party awaited him. But, unlike the wild activity accompanying his cousin John's wedding, the event transpired peacefully. A pastor from the nearby town of Goshen was willing to conduct the ceremony at the Gold home. Harriet's brother Stephen worked at his mill job during the service.

Colonel Gold and his wife accompanied the newlyweds for the first part of their journey to ensure safety. Harriet told her parents she rejoiced at the prospect of joining the Cherokees, but understood what lay ahead. "I think I may reasonably expect many trials, hardships, and privations."

As promised and warned, the trustees of the Cornwall Mission School closed down the school a few months later. The official reason cited was the perception that students were getting adequate training in other parts of the country. Although Rev. Stone refused to perform the wedding, he nevertheless was removed from his position at First

Church. He claimed the marriage as the reason for his demise.[4]

Elias and Harriet traveled to Philadelphia on their way home. At the First Presbyterian Church, he gave an address that remains one of the greatest speeches by a Native American ever recorded. The Cherokee Nation was now building momentum with the American people and its chief executive. Tangible evidence of their civilization included the proposed Constitution, their new capital city, the *Cherokee Phoenix* newspaper, and other specifics named by Boudinot: 41 mills, 62 blacksmith shops, 18 schools, 18 ferries, and thousands of books in personal libraries.

"You behold here an Indian," he began as his new wife listened from the congregation. "My fathers sleeping in the wilderness grave—they too were Indians. But I am not as my fathers were—broader means and nobler influences have fallen upon me. Yet I was not born as thousands are, in a stately dome and amid the congratulations of the great. For on a little hill, in a lonely cabin, overspread by the forest oak, I first drew my breath. And in a language unknown to learned and polished nations, I learnt to lisp my fond mother's name."

"What is an Indian?" he asked. "Is he not formed of the same materials with yourself? For of one blood God created all the nations that dwell on the face of the earth.

Though it be true that he is ignorant, that he is a heathen, that he is a savage, yet he is not more than all others have been under similar circumstances. Eighteen centuries ago what were the inhabitants of Great Britain?"

"The stale remark, 'Do what you will, an Indian will still be an Indian,' must be placed no more in speech," he said. "It must no longer be uttered, except by those who are uninformed with respect to us, who are strongly prejudiced against us, or who are filled with vindictive feelings towards us. The Cherokees most incontrovertibly establish the fallacy of this remark."

He continued speaking with allusions to the phoenix metaphor in the title of his newspaper: "I can view my native country, rising from the ashes of her degradation, wearing her purified and beautiful garments, and taking her seat with the nations of the earth."

Boudinot was pleading for public support, political support, and financial aid from his Christian brethren. "She will become not great, but a faithful ally of the United States. In times of peace she will plead the common liberties of America. In times of war her intrepid sons will sacrifice their lives in your defense. And because she will be useful to you in coming time, she asks you to assist her in her present struggles. She asks not for greatness. She seeks not wealth. She pleads only for assistance to become respectable as a nation, to enlighten and ennoble her sons, and to ornament her daughters with modesty and virtue."

Boudinot had no doubt that his nation, like Tecumseh before, was leading the other tribes in their quest for survival.

"She pleads for assistance, too, because on her destiny hangs that of many nations. If she complete her civilization, then we may hope that all our nations will," he said. "But if the Cherokee Nation fail in her struggle, if she die away, then all hopes are blasted, and falls the fabric of Indian civilization."

There are two alternatives, he said. "They must either become civilized and happy, or, sharing the fate of many kindred nations, become extinct. If the general government continue its protection, and the American people assist them in their humble efforts, they will, they must rise. Yes, under such protection, and with such assistance, the Indian must rise like the Phoenix."

And if the Americans do not assist them? Then the Cherokees and the tribes watching them "will go the way that so many tribes have gone before them. For the hordes that still linger about the shores of Huron, and the tributary streams of the Mississippi, will share the fate of those tribes that once lorded it along the proud banks of the Hudson; of that gigantic race that are said to have existed on the borders of the Susquehanna; of those various nations that flourished about the Potomac and the Rhappahannoc, and that peopled the forests of the vast valley Shenandoah. They will vanish like a vapor from the face of the earth, their very history will be lost in forgetfulness, and the places that now know them will know them no more.

"Shall this precedent be followed? I ask you, shall red men live, or shall they be swept away from the earth? With you and this public at large, the decision chiefly rests. Must they perish? Must they go down in sorrow to their graves?

"They hang upon your mercy as to a garment. Will you push them from you, or will you save them? Let humanity answer."[5]

CHAPTER ELEVEN

THE OBSTACLES

The proposed Cherokee Constitution placed President John Quincy Adams in a position that could threaten his reelection.

He succeeded James Monroe in 1824 after he and Andrew Jackson failed to garner the necessary electoral votes. The decision was thrown to the House of Representatives, who chose Adams. Jackson continued to grow in popularity, and any response to the Cherokees that southern states might perceive as a threat to their sovereignty would likely undo Adams politically.

Georgia had already flaunted the President's authority six months after the Cherokee Constitution was proposed in 1826. Former Creek Principal Chief William McIntosh, now broken by the tribe, had signed a treaty with federal authorities ceding a large portion of the tribe's land. The treaty gave the tribe two years to remove West, but excited settlers moved in immediately. The state of Georgia then officially began surveying the land in defiance of the treaty's time line, daring Adams to call in federal troops to force the issue.

Adams deliberated. Meanwhile, the Creeks dealt with McIntosh. At daylight, a band of 200 Creek warriors surrounded the former chief's large home. The house was set ablaze and his wife and children were allowed to escape. As McIntosh ran down the stairs with rifle in hand, he was met with a volley of bullets. He was dragged from the fire onto the lawn where fifty more rounds were fired into his head. He was then stabbed in the heart with a long knife.

General Edmund Gaines reported to the President that the Creeks, coached by Major Ridge and John Ridge, protested the treaty and planned to engage in civil disobedience. "They will make no sort of resistance, but will sit down quietly and be put to death where the bones of their ancestors are deposited: that the world shall know the Muscogee nation so loved their country that they were willing to die in it rather than sell it or leave it."[1]

The language foreshadowed actions that would soon be taken by thousands of the Cherokee people. But Adams was able to successfully negotiate a treaty with the Creeks soon after the McIntosh execution. He then announced he would send in federal troops to enforce the treaty time line.

Georgia pulled out the surveyors before an incident occurred, but responded instead with a bitter legislative resolution. They pronounced their sovereignty over the larger and more important territory of the Cherokees, who had signed no treaty, but had, instead, defiantly drafted their own Constitution.

The Cherokees had problems on another front: their unity was in danger. A large populist movement arose in opposition to ratifying the proposed Constitution, led by the ancient chief White Path, who fought with the Ridge under Dragging Canoe and with Andrew Jackson against the Redsticks.

White Path and his followers, such as Rising Fawn and Big Tiger, who still wore silver arm bracelets, warned against the teaching of the missionaries and against moving too quickly toward the customs of the white man. Laws against conjuring and ballplays were questioned, as were strict Sabbath regulations.

They may have also reacted to constitutional advocates like Boudinot. He believed the Cherokees had always been monotheists: "They cannot be called idolaters, for they never worshiped images. They believed in a Supreme Being, the Creator of all, the God of the white, the red, and the black man." Boudinot praised the modern Cherokees for outlawing polygamy, upholding female chastity, instituting Sabbath regulations, and ending tribal murder and the killing of witches.

White Path and his followers were uncomfortable with the swift changes. "It was not a question of selling the land of the Cherokees," said historian William McLoughlin, "but of selling their souls."

Delegates were elected from ten districts for ratification of the proposed Constitution. A follower of White Path named Kelachulee tied John Ridge in his district. According to the missionaries, the opposition caused a great stir. But Ross assured them it would not prevail: "A noise which will result in noise only," he said.

Indeed, White Path and his traditionalist party ultimately worked through their differences with the more progressive leaders. The Cherokees formed a united front and ratified their Constitution on July 4, 1827.[2]

After months of delay, President Adams finally issued a response to the Cherokees' founding document. He said it did not affect the federal government's relationship to the Cherokees. But he also made it clear they were not an independent, sovereign state: "It cannot be considered in any other light than as regulations of a purely municipal character," he said.

The Cherokees were actually pleased with the statement. "A pleasant surprise," wrote Boudinot in the *Phoenix*. Ross said the Constitution was never intended to exert an independence "unwarranted by the Treaties with the United States."

And that was the real issue. As McLoughlin writes: "Ross was well aware that Andrew Jackson and the western states believed that Indian treaty relationships with the federal government were the great stumbling block to Indian removal. Only an assertion of states rights against and above those of the federal government could ultimately attain the goal of those favoring total compulsory removal.

"The Cherokees had now maneuvered white America into a corner. To drive the Cherokees off their homeland, the whites would have to subvert their own Constitution."[3]

The Cherokees had now reached perhaps their highest level of political respect. They were unified. They had a legitimate government charter and a new capital city. Their people were growing more literate and more prosperous. And the President of the United States was committed to their rights under federal treaties.

But that still wasn't enough to satisfy the state of Georgia and the many American settlers who yearned for more land. The sentiment was captured by a popular song of the time:

All I ask in this creation
Is a pretty little wife and a big plantation
Way up yonder in the Cherokee Nation.[4]

Those same Americans also voiced their wishes at the ballot box. Only a few months after John Quincy Adams issued his statement on the Cherokee Constitution, he was defeated in his reelection bid.

The Cherokees' destiny was now in the hands of a United States federal government headed by a new leader—President Andrew Jackson.

CHAPTER TWELVE

THE PRESIDENT

Young Andrew Jackson fought in the revolution against the British and was captured at the age of thirteen. A few days before, his sixteen-year-old brother Hugh died in battle, and Andrew and his brother Robert found themselves inside a house that had been surrounded and then ransacked by enemy soldiers.

One of them instructed Andrew to wipe his boots. "Sir, I am a prisoner of war and claim to be treated as such," the boy replied. The soldier slashed him, but Andrew blunted the sword with his hand. The scars on his head and hand remained visible the rest of his life.

His father died while Andrew was still in the womb. His mother, Elizabeth, was known as a fierce opponent of the British and of the Indians who also threatened the lives of her friends and family.

An exchange of prisoners allowed Elizabeth to bring her two minor children home. She put the dying Robert on horseback while Andrew was left to walk forty-five miles barefoot without a jacket.

Robert died two days later. While Andrew recovered, his patriot mother traveled 160 miles to Charleston to nurse more colonial soldiers. She contacted cholera and died. Jackson never forgave the British.

Andrew Jackson inherited those qualities often attached to his Scotch-Irish ancestors: he was honest, truthful, stubborn, persistent, and impetuous. He rarely forgot an offense and carried a grudge to inordinate lengths. He considered William Wallace a hero for his "truly undaunted courage, always ready to brave any dangers."

The teenage orphan soon became known as "the most roaring, rollicking, game-cocking, horse-racing, card-playing, mischievous fellow" in his town. "A fighting cock all his life," writes biographer Robert Remini, "he was very kind to the hens who clucked around him but a savage killer toward any other cock who dared cross him."

He was tall and narrow with a pronounced jaw. His sandy hair was long and bushy and often stood straight upward. But his most notable feature was his bright, intensely blue eyes that blazed whenever passion seized him. "More than anything else, his eyes, when ignited, had a powerful effect on those around him," writes Remini. "They riveted attention; they commanded obedience; and they could terrorize."

Indians on the frontier were some of the first to experience his terror. When, as a young lawyer, he moved to Nashville, Tennessee—the furthest outpost west in the country—no one dared venture more than five miles outside the area. Indeed, a settler was killed by the native population every ten days.

Later, Jackson would articulate his view of the threat: "Brave Tennesseans, your frontier is threatened with invasion by a savage foe! Already they do advance towards your frontier, with their scalping knives unsheathed, to butcher our wives, your children, and your helpless babes."

He seemed to have a sixth sense as the "great Indian fighter of Tennessee."[1] After surviving a duel with another lawyer on the way to Nashville, he and his travelers camped in the woods. But Jackson was awakened by the sounds of the night.

"The owls," he said to a colleague. "Isn't that a little too natural?"

He then insisted that his sleepy friends get up immediately, because Indians surrounded them. "I know it," he said. "They mean to attack by daybreak."

Later that night, a party of white hunters found the still smoldering fires and claimed Jackson's former campsite. They were slaughtered at dawn.

Jackson soon became the local prosecutor. In time, he joined the ranks of the successful land speculators and owned tens, perhaps, hundreds of thousands of acres. He engaged in horse racing and traded horses, tobacco, and slaves. He promoted states rights with a vengeance, always writing united with a small *u* and States with a capital *S*.

Later, his wife Rachel experienced a strong religious conversion to which Jackson showed great respect. Her minister eventually became former chaplain Gideon Blackburn, whose whiskey escapades ended his mission work to the Cherokees. The Presbyterian preacher had also become a land speculator and an advocate for Indian removal.

Elected to the U.S. Congress, Jackson criticized the aristocratic "neebobs" in the senate. Later, as a senator, he was unusually quiet. One of his only recorded statements is a virulent protest against orders from the War Department not to wage war against the Indians unless attacked.[2]

In 1812, all eyes turned to the head of the Tennessee militia, General Andrew Jackson, who faced the British in New Orleans. President Madison and his wife Dolly were forced to leave the White House as British soldiers burned down the mansion, the federal arsenal, the Capitol, and the treasury buildings. Legislatures in New England were already debating the possibility of terms of surrender with the mother country. If Britain were able to take New Orleans and strangle the American continent, the war was over.

But Jackson won a forceful victory and gained hero status in America overnight. His victories over the Redstick Creeks added to the admiration from fellow American settlers who feared the threat of Indian attacks.

Jackson himself, always motivated since childhood to protect America from European enemies, saw the Indian tribes as a clear threat—always vulnerable to being seduced by Britain, France, or Spain to war against the Americans. "Treaties answer no other purpose than opening an easy door for the Indians to pass through and butcher our citizens," he said. He called peace talks "delusions."[3]

Americans loved Jackson for his sense of frontier justice. As one observer put it, his decisions were "short, untechnical, unlearned, ungrammatical, and generally right."

While serving as a Supreme Court justice for Tennessee, Jackson and the jury were cursed by a large man named Russell Bean who was accused of cutting off his infant's ears in a drunken frolic. Jackson commanded the bailiff to seize the hulking figure. But Bean slipped out of the simple one room courthouse in Knoxville as the sheriff ran after him.

The sheriff returned two minutes later.

"I couldn't catch him, your honor."

Jackson was not pleased. "Summon a posse, then, and bring him before me."

The judge hurried through the docket—he was known for trying several cases a day. An hour later, the sheriff entered the courthouse again, empty-handed.

"We couldn't apprehend him, your honor. He said he'd kill the first skunk what came within ten feet of him."

The justice's blue eyes blazed with even more intensity, adding to the fiery look from his frazzled hair. He controlled his fury and spoke with an even pace.

"Since you cannot obey my orders, summon me."

The law enforcement official gave him a confused look.

"Yes, sir. Summon me!"

"Well, judge, if you say so. I don't like to do this," said the sheriff, but "I suppose I must summon you."

"Very well," said Jackson. "I adjourn this court ten minutes." He ripped off his black robe and walked out the door.

The audacious Russell Bean was now brandishing his weapons in the town square and shouting curses to a gathering crowd. The chief justice grabbed a pistol in each hand and walked straight toward the criminal. The crowd cleared out of the way.

"Now, surrender you infernal villain, this very instant, or I'll blow you through."

Bean stared into his eyes, motionless. He lowered his weapon, then dropped it to the ground.

"It's no use judge," he said. "I give in."

Jackson ordered him apprehended and thrown in jail.

A few days later, Bean was asked why he surrendered to Jackson after defying an entire posse.

"When he came up, I looked him in the eye and I saw shoot," Bean said, "and there wasn't shoot in nary other eye in the crowd."[4]

The Georgians knew Jackson had "shoot" in his eye for all opponents of removal. A month after the presidential election, and several weeks before Jackson took office, the Georgia legislature passed a sweeping series of laws. They pronounced the Cherokee territory as now under the complete sovereignty of the state of Georgia.

All Cherokee laws were declared nullified. All Cherokee assemblies or meetings of the council were forbidden. Any Cherokee who influenced a fellow tribesman against removal would be arrested. Contracts between Indians and whites were null and void unless witnessed by two whites. No Indian was allowed to testify in court against a white man.

Digging for gold was also strictly prohibited. That law became especially relevant with the discovery of the precious metal in Cherokee country at Dahlonega, Georgia. Hordes of white frontiersmen had already swarmed over the land in search of their fortunes. The timing of the discovery of gold only added fuel to the desires to seize all Cherokee property.

New York Congressman Edward Everett argued that unprincipled whites could now legally steal the land. "They have but to choose the time and the place, where the eye of no white man can rest upon them, and they may burn the dwelling, waste the farm, plunder the property, assault the person, and murder the children of the Cherokee subject of Georgia," he said. "And though hundreds of the tribe may be looking on, there is not one of them that can be permitted to bear witness against the spoiler."

This tactic soon was tried on several wealthy Cherokees, including Major Ridge, whose property included a plantation and large home, a ferry, orchards, and much livestock. His signature was forged on a note, and the whites relied on the new law to allow them to secure the property. At this point, however, the jury was unwilling to rule against the chief—some elements of the Georgia public still resented the obvious injustice. "We cannot omit to express ourselves decidedly hostile to the law excluding Indians from the privilege of testifying in our courts," opined the *Georgia Journal*. "It is unjust, and inexpedient and should be repealed."

Most incidents never made it to court. One band of settlers, unable to find the assets they wanted on the property of an old woman, set fire to her grove and sat in their saddles laughing as she scrambled to save her fence.

These "Pony Clubs" roved the land, seizing hogs, horses, and cattle. Some of them squatted down on large tracts of land belonging to the Indians.

Eventually, the Cherokees reached the breaking point in their decades-long policy of refusing to take up arms. Since the time of Dragging Canoe, they had chosen to fight as "civilized" men in courts of law. And by treaty they deferred to the whites the job of punishing any border violations on either side. After Tecumseh's proposal to use force, they continued to choose the rule of law over frontier warfare.

They met at Ross's home and determined to take a police action against a group of settlers who had squatted on a settlement at Beaver Dam near the Georgia–Alabama line. Jackson's friend General Coffee was also there, sent to convince them to choose removal to prevent further pillaging. But after hearing both sides, Coffee found himself sympathetic to the Cherokee dilemma. A police action would not violate the rule of law, he said. Because of the latest developments, the Principal Chief now had the duty to enforce the border laws.

Major Ridge was appointed to lead sixty soldiers to remove the settlers. To add to the effect, the Ridge enhanced his usual modern dress by wearing a buffalo-horned headdress—an item he likely acquired from Boudinot who had begun collecting such traditional items from around the nation for a new Cherokee museum. The other soldiers colored their faces for effect.

Their numbers overwhelmed the eighteen families, who they ordered to evacuate immediately. After giving them plenty of time to do so, Ridge ordered the homes and buildings that had been originally built by Cherokees to be burned.

Georgia papers condemned the act. Governor Gilmer seized the opportunity: "A number of women, with infant children, were thus deprived of shelter." Bands of armed white men threatened to burn down the homes of Ridge and Ross, and throngs of Indians grabbed rifles to defend their leaders. "War in Georgia," proclaimed papers in the North.[5]

CHAPTER THIRTEEN
THE BLOOD LAW

It took little time for the seasoned Cherokee leaders to decide they had made a strategic mistake. Boudinot editorialized their reversal: "[This is] a circumstance we have for a long time dreaded," he said. "It has been the desire of our enemies that the Cherokees may be urged to some desperate act. But we would say, Forbear, forbear—revenge not, but leave vengeance to him 'to whom vengeance belongeth.'"

Leaving justice to white America's commitment to the rule of law became more difficult for many Cherokees. Even the clerk of the National Council, Alexander McCoy, had his property at New Echota evaluated by an emigration agent. For this defection he was stripped of his post and replaced by John Ridge.

Because of such actions, the chiefs met on October 24, 1829, to draw up a drastic measure to prevent acts of treason in the nation. The "Blood Law" pronounced death to any betrayers:

"Whereas a law has been in existence for many years, but not committed to writing, that if any citizen or citizens of this nation should treat or dispose of any lands belonging to this nation without special permission from the national authorities, he or they shall suffer death."[1]

All the great leaders attended this solemn council and believed such a measure would help their cause. Very soon, however, certain leading chiefs would deeply regret it.

With the force of arms no longer an option, the Cherokees placed their hopes on Congress refusing to pass Jackson's Indian Removal Bill. This was the President's first and most important piece of legislation, on which he had placed the success of his entire administration.

Jackson always considered himself the great friend of the Indians. He pointed to the fate of the Mohegans, Delawares, and Narragansetts. They were now extinct. The same will happen to the Southern Indians, he said. But his removal plan would save them. "No man entertains kinder feelings toward the Indians than Andrew Jackson," declared Georgia House member Wilson Lumpkin, who later became Governor.

"I have no motive, Brothers, to deceive you," Jackson assured the Cherokees. But he did think his opponents were deceived and warned them not to oppose him. "I leave the poor deluded Creeks and Cherokees to their fate, and their annihilation," he said.

The bill was hotly contested, "as protracted and excited as any that had ever before taken place," said Senator Martin Van Buren. Another congressman said it was one of the severest debates he had ever witnessed.

Representative Henry Storrs of New York articulated the stakes: only Congress had the power to stop Jackson. And this was their one moment to do so: "If these encroachments of the Executive Department are not met and repelled in these halls," he shouted, "they will be resisted nowhere."[2]

Representative Edward Everett of Massachusetts sensed the condemnation of future generations if they did not prevail: "When the interest and passion of the day are past, [we] shall look back on it, I fear, with self reproach and a regret as bitter as unavailing."

He called for a "grand council-fire" where all the past treaties with the Indians could be burned in the face of day. "Many of them were negotiated under the instructions of Washington, of Adams, of Jefferson—the fathers of our liberty," he said. "But our present Chief Magistrate, as he lays them, one by one, on the fire, will see his own name subscribed to a goodly number of them. Sir, they ought to be destroyed as a warning to the Indians to make no more compacts with us."

John Ridge and a colleague sat in the gallery listening to his speech. In front of them was a writer for the *New York Observer*, who listened to Everett's stirring words as well. "Two of the Cherokees stood immediately behind me and over me," he said. "I thought I heard something like a drop of rain fall upon my cloak, near my ear. I looked up, and the head of one of the Cherokees had fallen upon his hand, and he was endeavoring to conceal his tears."[3]

Popular Tennessee Congressman Davy Crockett may have lightened the days of heavy-hearted debate with his satirical amendment to the bill. A legendary Indian advocate, Crockett proposed the removal of all whites from eastern Tennessee to beyond the Mississippi, lest they impede on the territorial designs and sovereignty of Georgia.

The results of removal for those Cherokees who had already removed west provided no encouragement to the Eastern Cherokee leaders. Settlers had gotten around the other side of the Cherokees in Arkansas and were grabbing land on their western border as well as their eastern side. The Arkansas settlers now seemed as intent on removing their Indians further west as the Georgians were to remove them from the East. Calhoun had actually encouraged the Arkansas Cherokees to move further west, but they refused. These developments proved "the uselessness of this emigration scheme," wrote Boudinot.

As Congress deliberated, another important group also weighed heavily on the political question. The missionaries had become hotly divided over how they should or should not speak out on the issue of removal.

Worcester's mentor, Jeremiah Evarts, a member of the American Mission Board, wrote a series of articles under the name William Penn in which he condemned removal. Georgia's Lumpkin quoted Evarts with contempt that he would so disrespect the civil government. "Better that half the states were annihilated and the rest left powerful in holiness, than the whole nation be stained by this guilt," Evarts said. "We would rather have a civil war, were there no other alternative, than avoid it by taking shelter in a crime."[4]

Worcester took his mentor's words to heart. Little did he know how relevant they would soon become for the missionaries at Brainerd and New Echota.

But Representative Lumpkin fumed over missionaries like Evarts and Worcester. He denounced the "wicked influence of designing men veiled in the garb of philanthropy and Christian benevolence." They were "fanatics . . . flocking in upon the poor Cherokees, like the caterpillars and locusts of Egypt."

Eventually, Jackson supporters were successful in eliminating the federal monies that helped build facilities at Indian missions like Brainerd. That did not stop Worcester. He fortified opponents of removal in Congress with a long and informative statement about Cherokee progress and the large number of converts to the Christian religion.

Later, Worcester took the bold step of calling a conference of missionaries from all denominations to prepare a joint statement on the issue. He had written Boston for official clearance to speak out politically, despite the push from many quarters to stay out of politics and focus on saving souls.

Some opponents were close to home. Missionary Butrick searched the New Testament and in Acts found that many times the apostles found flocks suffering from political persecution but did not address it, for the kingdom of heaven is not of this world.

The idealistic Butrick, who had early on taken a vow of celibacy, now had another reason to avoid possible persecution. He had married. During the discussions of a Cherokee Constitution in 1827, Butrick wrote the mission board for wisdom on whether he should keep his early vow.

But by the time the response came, the issue was already settled. On his way to preach at a mission, he found Elizabeth Proctor all alone with her male scholars. "Dear loves, said I, how can I leave them immediately alone in this wild desert?" So he stayed the night. However, he became conscience-stricken over the propriety of the situation, but his horse ran away and a neighbor nearby had no room. The only way to solve the dilemma and protect Elizabeth's reputation, he said, was to marry her. She was willing.

Butrick gained a brother-in-law in the process, and he and Isaac Proctor had misgivings about Worcester's political enthusiasm. Nevertheless, the board approved of the joint statement set forth by the four denominations, represented by twelve missionaries who met at Worcester's home in New Echota. The eight-point manifesto condemned the removal issue and said Georgia's enactment of jurisdiction over Cherokee lands was injurious to the nation. "If we withheld our opinions when called for, we could not hold up our heads as preachers of righteousness among a people who would universally regard us as abettors of iniquity," explained the missionaries.

Butrick begrudgingly joined his colleagues: "We must sign the document prepared or be censured as unfriendly to the Cherokees," he wrote privately to a friend. "In my opinion, the Cherokees should never have been taught to expect political aid from missionaries."

Elias Boudinot immediately ran a special "extra" edition of the *Cherokee Phoenix* in which the entire manifesto was printed in English and Sequoyan. "We believe no one can now remain neutral," he wrote. "Each individual in America must now be for the Indians or against them."[5]

While the American Mission Board stood strong against removal, the Cherokee leaders provided a united front across the nation. John Ross, Major Ridge, John Ridge, Elias Boudinot, and others rode tirelessly across the land encouraging their people to remain strong and resist the pressures to remove.

A statement sent to Washington, D.C., from several chiefs is generally attributed to Major Ridge and John: "We are now assaulted with menaces of expulsion, because we have unexpectantly become civilized, and because we have formed and organized a constituted government. It is too much for us now to be honest, and virtuous, and industrious, because then we are capable to aspiring to the rank of Christians and politicians, which renders our attachment to the soil more strong, and therefore more difficult to defraud us of our possession."

"We hereby individually set our faces to the rising sun, and turn our backs to its setting. As our ancestors revered the sepulchral monuments of the noble dead, we cherish the sacred spots of their repose, under hillocks of clay that cover them from sight."[6]

Such memorials to Congress made their impact. One amendment to overturn the removal bill gained significant momentum. The vote was tied, but the Speaker voted against it. With added pressure from the White House, several Democratic members from Pennsylvania and Massachusetts were whipped into line. When the bill came up again, it passed 102 to 97.

Congressman Freulinghuysen pronounced the bill the United States' answer to this simple question: "How shall we most plausibly break our faith?"

Frances Milton Trallope, a British woman who attended the debates, was struck by the contradiction between principle and practice in America. "You will see them with one hand hoisting the cap of liberty, and with the other flogging their slaves," she wrote. "You will see them one hour lecturing their mob on the indefeasible rights of men, and the next driving from their homes the children of the soil, whom they have bound themselves to protect by the most solemn treaties."

However, the language of the bill contained one hopeful clause: " . . . provided that nothing in this act shall be construed as authorizing the violation of any existing treaty between the United States and any Indian tribes."[7] The

Cherokees needed an opportunity to test the new law in the Supreme Court by some particular victim of Georgia's laws.

But the Cherokees now faced a threat that could end their ability to stand firm amid the chaos on their borders and in the courts.

A week after Worcester and the missionaries wrote their manifesto at New Echota, they received word that Georgia passed another law. It was now illegal and punishable by imprisonment for any white man to remain in Cherokee territory—unless he took an oath of allegiance to the state of Georgia.

Threatened with arrests, imprisonment, and hard labor, the missionaries considered whether to remain in the Cherokee Nation.

CHAPTER FOURTEEN

THE ARRESTS

Major Ridge was present at the mission house of Butrick and his brother-in-law, Isaac Proctor, when a copy of the January 1, 1831, *Georgia Journal* was delivered with the news that Georgia would imprison the missionaries if they remained.

Proctor told Ridge that the missionaries should leave Georgia and move over to Tennessee territory. He even hinted to Boston that his service may be more valuable now in New England. Butrick continued to argue that Christians should surrender to the state on all temporal matters.

The Scripture at issue came from Romans 13 in the New Testament: "Let every soul be subject unto higher powers. For there is no power but of God. The powers that be are ordained of God. Whoever therefore resisteth the power, resisteth the ordinance of God: and they that resist shall receive unto themselves damnation."

Butrick wrote Elias Boudinot on the matter and said a missionary must submit to the higher power of President Jackson: "If the President should decide that we are not under the protection of the [Federal] Government, we should do so," he said.

Principal Chief John Ross told Boudinot the opposite: "I do hope our white citizens will not be so ignorant of their own rights to be frightened . . . and expatriate themselves by licking the usurper's hand."

Butrick informed the American Mission Board in Boston he was moving and establishing residence across the border in Tennessee.

Worcester also wrote the Board: "I cannot view it but as a matter of regret that our ranks are broken," he said. But Worcester had another view of the higher power: "The Cherokee government was of rightful authority," he argued, because the treaties gave them authority to govern themselves according to their own laws. It would take a decision of the Supreme Court to convince Worcester otherwise, not simply the policy of the sitting President.[1]

The Cherokees hired the former attorney general under James Monroe to take such a case to the highest court. William Wirt, a neighbor of Thomas Jefferson and the lawyer who prosecuted Aaron Burr, selected a case in the Georgia courts of an Indian named George Tassels, accused of murder and scheduled for hanging.

Georgia did not appear before the court when Wirt argued the case, showing their disdain for the notion of the Cherokee Nation's legitimacy before the justices. Wirt not only hoped to free Tassels from execution, but more importantly, for the Court to use the case to determine that all of Georgia's laws over the Cherokees were invalid.

"They assumed our dress, copied our names, pursued our course of education, adopted our form of government, embraced our religion, and have been proud to imitate us in everything in their power," Wirt argued as he spoke before the justices. He then celebrated their noble leaders, specifically referring to the Ridge: "They were once the lords of the forest—men worthy to associate with the 'lion,' who, in their own language, 'walks upon the mountain tops.' They fought side by side with our present chief magistrate, and received his personal thanks for their gallantry and bravery."[2]

John Ridge and his friends attended the trial that day in Washington. They knew that Chief Justice John Marshall, a longtime rival of Jackson, was sympathetic to their cause. They were hopeful for a positive decision.

It took Marshall twenty-five minutes to deliver the decision. He spoke in a soft and quavering voice, and the crowd was forced to move forward to understand him. It was soon clear that the Cherokees had been denied.

Marshall explained that they had sued as a foreign nation, which was not their proper legal status. Rather, they were a "domestic, dependent nation . . . in a state of pupilage."

The Cherokees, however, chose to view the interpretation in a positive light. They would sue again as a domestic, dependent nation. They even received a private letter from Marshall encouraging them to do so.

Jackson, on the other hand, viewed the decision as a victory for his side. When a delegation of Cherokees led by John Ridge visited him just after the decision, he reminded them of his strong position: "I knew that your claims before the Supreme Court would not be supported," he said. "The court has sustained my views in regard to your nation."

Then, in his usual manner, he expressed his devotion to them and his desire to do the best for them. "I am particularly glad to see you at this time," he said. "I am a friend of the Cherokees. They fought with me in the war and freely shed their blood with the blood of my soldiers in defending the United States. How could I be otherwise than their friend?"

Ridge strongly denied reports that the Cherokees were despondent over Marshall's decision. And when a Georgia news story questioned whether Ridge's delegation may have angered the President, John replied: "Sooner than ask the President if he were angry with me, I would cut my tongue out."[3]

John Ross and the council were also pleased with the decision. The phrase "domestic and dependent nation" at least identified the Cherokees as a nation and not as tenants at will in the state of Georgia. A second Supreme Court case was now required to determine their exact rights under this legal status.

At New Echota, Rev. Worcester waited patiently for a reply from Boston on how to proceed regarding the oath to Georgia. Meanwhile, Georgia settlers and officials continued to harass Cherokees on their lands. Dahlonega was filled with treasure hunters, most of whom did not find what they wanted and pressed further into Cherokee country to find their fortune in Indian land.

Indian Agent Hugh Montgomery, no Cherokee partisan, said several thousand "gamblers, swindlers, and debauchers" were plaguing the area in search of gold. "Their morals are as bad as it is possible for you to conceive," he told a colleague. "Think of Sodom before the arrival of the destroying angels, and you have some faint idea of the morals of the place."

John Ridge reported in the *Phoenix* that Georgians murdered twenty Creeks on the Cherokee frontier. "Who now are the savages?" he demanded. "No pity or shame seems to go with their designs, as if we were wolves or boa constrictors."

Boudinot was an open-minded editor. He willingly printed a response to his cousin's letter from a Ralph Scrugg of Gainesville. He called John a "damned little frog eater and wasp destroyer" and expressed a desire to cut strips from his back for use in making a horsewhip. "If you don't mind, I will sell you as a Negro," he added, "for you favor one more than a damned Indian."

It was generally useless to alert the Georgia authorities. In one instance, three members of the Georgia Guard charged into a river after witnessing a group of Cherokees receive baptism. They said they felt the Spirit as well, and baptized their horses with full rites. Boudinot editorialized on the blasphemy in the *Phoenix*.

Besides the threat of arrest, Worcester faced other serious problems. His wife Ann had fallen dangerously ill. Doctors could not make the trip to New Echota. Samuel had to nurse his wife as best as he could, but she could not sit up without fainting. She was expecting her third child.

But she never wavered in her support for the Cherokee cause. In his letter to Boston, Worcester asked if his wife should remain to run the mission if he were arrested. "Mrs. Worcester is perfectly ready to run the risk of being forcibly removed," he wrote.

When the American Mission Board's letter finally arrived, they wholeheartedly endorsed Worcester's position over Butrick's. "Taking the oath of allegiance is out the question," they said. They agreed that the land was legally under Cherokee jurisdiction, not Georgia's, and that the law should be ignored. Anything less would cause the Cherokees to doubt the sincerity of the missionaries. As a body they felt "called to suffer persecutions . . . for the sake of Christ and the gospel."[4]

Twelve days after the letter arrived, the missionaries were given the opportunity to practice their beliefs. Proctor was the first to be arrested, ironically, since he had not yet moved across the border. Three guards took him forty miles to New Echota where Worcester and three others were taken before a magistrate. They were treated carefully and released after the judge noted that Worcester was a postmaster for his area and therefore legally in residence as a federal agent. He was given early release to see his wife, who had just given birth to their third daughter.

It did not take Andrew Jackson long to remedy the situation. When the Georgia Governor asked the President about Worcester's status, Jackson ordered the missionary removed from his position as a postal agent.

It was clear to all now that another arrest would soon take place. The penalty for defying the oath statute was four years of hard labor in the penitentiary. Despite the difficult prospect, Worcester's mentor, Jeremiah Evarts, wrote with glowing enthusiasm for the opportunity to use such an arrest as the key case for the United States Supreme Court to test Georgia's laws.

"If Georgia should carry some of you to prison, the fact would rouse this whole country in a manner unlike anything which has yet been experienced," Evarts wrote, and then added more pressure. "If you leave, I fear the Cherokees will make no stand whatever."

Evarts wrote from Boston, but Rev. Samuel Worcester still resided in Georgia. It was he who would experience the pain that Evarts believed to be such an opportunity.

Worcester wondered if any other missionaries were willing to give such a sacrifice for the Cherokees. Even if they did not, he made up his mind. "If all my brethren forsake me, I am willing to bear the burden alone," he wrote back to Boston. "Only let not God forsake me."

Butrick, however, was not willing to join Worcester in the act of civil disobedience. And he told Boston he believed he too had the correct Christian stance: "It has appeared to me to be more like suffering in a political contest, from motives of worldly policy, than in the spirit of Christian meekness."[5]

Butrick and Proctor were safely on Tennessee soil when the next arrests were made. This time, the Georgia Guard was not gentle.

On July 7, Worcester was arrested along with ten other missionaries, including Dr. Elizur Butler, who was forced to walk chained by the neck to the neck of a guardsman's horse. "They were dragged with bleeding feet, through the rough and tangled forest," wrote John Ridge, "at the point of a bayonet, and even in sickness. With wounded feet, they were refused the privilege of riding their horses."

A Methodist missionary who protested his arrest was beaten over the head with a stick by the Georgia Guard and was forced to march sixty miles to the prison.

A Sergeant Brooks was the leader in hurling insults at the missionaries, curses which Worcester said could not be any more obscene. In a mocking tone, he parodied the voice of Jesus: "Fear not, little flock, for it is the Father's good pleasure to give you the Kingdom."

They were marched into Camp Gilmer to the sound of fife and drum. "There is where all the enemies of Georgia have to land," said Brooks as they entered. "There—and in hell!"

Their cell had a dirty floor and smelled. They made a few small holes in the wall for air and light and then slept on the floor.

"We have plenty of wholesome food and good water and a sufficient supply of blankets," Worcester reported from his cell. "We dwell in peace, and with peace of conscience we are contented."

As they attempted to rest, several guards lay down by their door to disturb their sleep. One re-echoed several times from the mouth of Brooks, "Fear not, little flock.'"

On July 21 they were released until their trial before the Georgia Supreme Court in September. Worcester rushed back to attend to his sickly wife, knowing that at any time he could be rearrested for the trial. The moment came the day after his infant child died. A sympathetic guard came to him in disguise the night before to warn him of the third arrest the next evening. Upon hearing of the death, however, the official in charge let him visit his wife for a while longer before being taken.

All eleven missionaries were sentenced to four years hard labor in the Milledgeville Penitentiary. It took the jury fifteen minutes to deliberate. The judge reminded them of their duty to obey God by obeying their rulers. When they were marched to the prison doors, they were informed of the Governor's offer to pardon them if they either took the oath or returned home and left the borders of Georgia. The iron doors were slowly opened so the creaking noise would add to the horror of imprisonment. Nine took the offer. Only Worcester and Butler remained.

The two remaining prisoners refused to acknowledge any guilt by accepting a pardon. They also knew that the Governor's action was an admission of his desire not to test the law in the U.S. Supreme Court.

Worcester took up carpentry in the jail while Butler practiced the shoemaker's trade. On Sunday, Worcester preached, and his sermons were well attended by fellow prisoners.[6]

ᏣᎳᎩ   ᏓᎳᏲᎯᎢ

CHEROKEE   PHŒNIX.

VOL. I.   NEW ECHOTA, THUESDAY MARCH 13, 1828.   NO. 4.

EDITED BY ELIAS BOUDINOTT,

ISAAC H. HARRIS,

FOR THE CHEROKEE NATION.

At $2 50 if paid in advance, $3 in six months, or $3 50 if paid at the end of the year.

To subscribers who can read only the English language the price will be $2,00 prepaid, or $2,50 to be paid within the year.

Every subscription will be considered as continued unless subscribers give notice to the contrary before the commencement of a new year.

The Phœnix will be printed on a Superroyal sheet, with type entirely new procured for the purpose. Any person procuring six subscribers, and becoming responsible for the payment, shall receive a seventh gratis.

Advertisements will be inserted at seventy-five cents per square for the first insertion, and thirty-seven and a half cents for each continuance; longer ones in proportion.

☞ All letters addressed to the Editor, post paid, will receive due attention.

ᎠᎴ ᏕᎦᎳ ᎠᎴ ᏥᏍᏆᏱ,
ᎤᎾᏘ ᎤᎾᎳᏓᎢ ᏪᏔᎾ ᎢᏳᎾᎵᏍᏔᏅᎢ,
ᏔᏪ ᎤᏣᎴ ᏕᎳᎾᎴᎦᎥᎢ, ᎤᏪ
ᏣᎦᏣᏱ ᏕᎳᎾᎦᎸᎯ, ᎤᎵᏓᏃ
ᏣᏔ ᏕᎳᎳᎾᎢ, ᏕᎦᏓᎳᎢᎥ ᎤᏣᎥ
ᏕᎦᏓ ᏕᎦᏓᎴᎢᏔᎢ, ᏔᏪ ᎤᎶᎾ
ᏕᎦᎾ ᏕᎳᎳᏃᏔ, ᎤᎾᏗ ᎤᏗᎳ Ꮤ
ᏕᎦᏔᏃᎢ

CHEROKEE LAWS.

The following laws of the Cherokee Nation we publish as we find them in print, without any corrections, except what we may get typographical errors. They already been circulated in this Nation in the Cherokee tongue—Our readers at a distance will perhaps be gratified to see the commencement of written laws among the Cherokees. The repealing laws will in the order as they were passed.

Be it known, That this day, the various clans or tribes which compose the Cherokee Nation, have unanimously passed an act of oblivion for all lives for which they may have been indebted one to the other, and have mutually agreed that after this evening the aforesaid act shall become binding upon every clan, or tribe; and the aforesaid clans or tribes have also agreed that if in future, any life should be lost without malice intended, the innocent aggressor shall not be accounted guilty.

Be it known also, That should it so happen that a brother, forgetting his natural affection, should raise his hand in anger and kill his brother, he shall be accounted guilty of murder and suffer accordingly. And if a man has a horse stolen, and overtakes the thief, and should his anger be so great as to cause him to kill him, let his blood remain on his own conscience, but no satisfaction shall be demanded for his life from his relatives or the clan he may belong to.

By order of the seven clans.

TURTLE AT HOME,
Speaker of Council.

Approved.

BLACK FOX, Principal Chief.
PATH KILLER, Scr'd.
TOOCHALAR.

CHARLES HICKS, Sec'y to the Council.

Oostanallah, April 10, 1810.

WHEREAS, fifty-four towns and villages having convened in order to deliberate and consider on the situation of our nation, in the disposition of our common property of lands without the unanimous consent of the members of the Council, and in order to obviate the evil consequences resulting in such course, we have unanimously adopted the following form for the future government of our nation.

ARTICLE 1st. It is unanimously agreed, that there shall be thirteen members elected as a Standing Committee for the term of two years, at the end of which term they shall be

ᎤᏣᏓᎳᎢ ᎤᏔᏓ ᎤᏯ ᏕᏓᎦᎢ
Ꭷ ᎤᏕ ᏕᏪᎤᎢ ᏕᎳᎳᎦ ᎤᎦ ᎤᎾᏆ
Ꮤ ᏃᎵ ᏕᎦᎵᎾᏆ ᏔᏪᎢ, ᏕᎦ ᎤᏆᎴ ᎤᏗᎢ
ᏕᎦᎾᎵ ᏔᏪᎦᏴᎤ ᏕᎦᎳᏔᎵᎾ ᏕᎳᎳᎾ
ᏔᏪ ᏕᎦᏆᎴᎢᎥᎢ. ᎠᎵ ᎤᏣᎴ ᏕᎳᏓᎾ
Ꮤ ᎤᏔᎴᎢᎥᎢ. ᎠᎵ ᎤᏔ ᎬᎴᎢ
Ꮤ ᏕᎳᎾ ᎤᎴ ᏃᏄᎢᏔᎢᎥᎢ. ᏔᏪ
Ꮤ ᏕᎦᎾ ᏕᎳᎳᎾᎾ. ᏔᏪ ᎤᏕ
Ꮤ ᏕᎦᎳᏓᎢᎥᎢ. ᏔᏪ ᏕᎦᎾᎾ
Ꮤ ᏕᎦᎾᎳᏓᎢᎥᎢ.

ᏕᎦᎾ ᎤᏣᏓᎳᎢᎥ ᏕᎦᎾ ᏕᎦᏣᎴᎢ,
ᏔᏪ ᏴᏕ ᎤᏔᎴ ᏕᎦ ᏔᏣᎾ ᏕᎦᎳᎢ,
ᏕᎳᎾ ᏔᎾᎤᎦᎳᏓ ᏕᎦ ᏔᎾᎤᏣᎴᎢ ᎤᎴ
ᏔᎦᏔᏪ, ᏕᎦ ᎤᎳᏓᎳᏗᎾ ᏔᎾᎢᎥᎢ. ᏔᎦᎴ
Ꮤ ᏕᎾᎳ ᏕᎦ ᏔᎾᎢᎥᎢ ᏔᎦᎳ ᎤᏣᎳ
ᏔᎢ ᏔᎦᏣ ᏔᎾᎾᏔ ᏔᎾᎤᎵᎾᎢᎥᎢ Ꮓ
ᏕᎵ ᎤᎾᏔ ᏕᎦᎴᎾᎢᎥ, ᏔᎵ ᎤᏣᎴ
ᏕᎳᏔ ᎤᎾᏔ ᏕᎦ ᏕᎵᎾ ᏕᎦᎾᎾᎢ

ᎤᏔᎾ ᏕᎳ.

ᏔᏪ, ᎤᎾᎴᎢ.

ᎤᎳᏔᎾ, ᎤᎾᎴᎢ ᎤᏓᏉ.
ᏕᎳᏔ 78 ᏔᎳᎵ, 1808.

ᏕᎳᎳᏔᎢ Ꮤ ᏔᏪ ᏃᏘ, ᎤᎵ ᎤᏣᎦᏆᎴ
ᏔᎾᏔᎢᏕ Ꮤ ᎤᏣᏔᎢ, ᏃᎵ ᎤᎾᎤ ᎤᏣᎾ
Ꮤ ᎤᎳᎾᎢᎥ Ꮤ ᎤᏣᎢ, ᏔᏪ ᎤᏣ ᎤᏣᎾ
ᏕᎳᎢ ᏃᎵ ᎤᏣᎳ ᏔᎾᎳᎳᎾ ᏔᎾᎤᎢ, ᎤᏣᎾ
Ꮤ ᎤᏔ ᎤᎴᏔᎢ ᏔᎦᎳᎾᎵᎾ ᏔᏪᎳᎢ

ᏔᏪ ᏕᎦᎾ, ᏔᎾᏓᎾ.
ᎤᎳᎵ, ᏔᏪᎳ ᏴᏔ ᏔᎵ.
ᏔᏪᎳᏔ.

ᎤᏔ, ᎤᎳᎢᏔᎾᎢ ᏕᎦᏴ ᏴᎤᎳ.
ᏕᎳᎳ, ᏴᏔ 78 ᏔᎵᎳᎢ, 1808.

ᏕᎦᎾᎳᎢ ᎤᏔᎴ ᏔᎵ, ᎤᏣ ᎤᏪᎴᎾ
ᏔᎾᎳᎢ Ꮓ ᏔᎾᎾᎢ, ᏔᎦᎾ ᎤᏔᎾ ᎤᏔᎾ
ᏔᎾᎳᎴ 78 ᏔᎾᎾᎢ, ᏔᎦ ᎤᏔᎾ ᎤᏔ ᎤᏣᎾ
ᎤᎾᎳ ᏕᎾᎳᎢ ᏔᏣᎳᎾᏔᎢ, ᎤᏣᎾ
Ꮤ ᎤᏔ ᎤᎳᎳᎾ ᏕᎦᎾᎢᎥ ᏔᎳᎢ. ᏔᎦ
ᎤᏣᎾ ᏔᎾᏆᎴ ᏔᎾᎴᎾ ᏔᎾᎳᎾ. ᏔᎾᎢᎥ
ᏕᎳ ᎤᏣᎾ ᏕᎦᎳᎳᎾᏔᎾᎢᎥᎾᎢ ᏔᎵ ᏔᎾ
ᏕᎳᎵ ᎤᏣ ᏔᎾᎾᏔ ᏃᎵ ᏕᎦᎳᎾᎢᎥ Ꮓ
ᎤᏔ.

ᏕᎳᎾ ᏔᎾᎳᎾ Ꮤ.
ᎤᏔᎳᎢ ᎤᏔᎾᏓᎾ, ᏕᎦ
ᏔᎴᎳᎾ ᏔᎾᏔ.
ᏕᎾ.

SCANDAL.

'There are people,' continued the corporal, 'who can't even breathe, without slandering a neighbor.'

'I'm judge too severely,' replied my aunt Prudy, 'no one is slandered who does not deserve it.'

'That may be,' retorted the corporal, 'but I have heard very slight things said of you.'

The face of my aunt kindled with anger. 'Me!' she exclaimed, 'slight things of me! what can any body say of me!'

'They say,' answered the corporal gravely, and drawing his words to keep her in suspense, 'that—that you are no better than you ought to be.'

Fars flashed from the

CHAPTER FIFTEEN

THE REBELLION

Ann Worcester took it upon herself to run the mission school in her husband's absence. She folded the copies of the unfinished New Testaments and hymnals that her husband had printed earlier. Harriet Boudinot, her next-door neighbor, helped with piano lessons, and they all sang gospel songs with the students in the living room.

Harriet wrote to her sisters regarding her love for Elias: "He is truly worthy of my warmest affections—my tenderest love," she said. "He works very hard."

John Ridge wrote to his white in-laws with a good report on his and Sarah's relationship: "My wife is very good to me and I love her dearly." He built her a fine house that he said would look well even in New England.

But he assured Sarah's parents that the Cherokees would defeat Jackson: "You may rest assured that our people will not yield to the policy of Jackson to gratify the cupidity of Georgia."

In one letter, Harriet was less confident: "We know not what is before us. Sometimes I fear the Cherokees will see evil days."[1]

Indeed, Elias was hauled up by the Georgia Guard twice for his "abusive and libelous articles" and threatened with flogging. But each time he was released.

Over 500 surveyors boldly traversed the Cherokee Nation, marking the land in 160-acre tracts for an upcoming lottery of Indian land. In Dahlonega, the valuable gold-laden tracts were only forty acres. No part of the Cherokee land was omitted for the lottery.

Ann Worcester noticed a former Baptist preacher surveying the land and confronted him about his actions. He apologized, saying he needed the money. But if he hadn't taken the job, someone else would have, he told her.

The missionary wife could take heart in the fact that her husband's suffering was awakening the country to the cause of the Cherokees. Even the Georgians were becoming divided, as evidenced by a literacy society that held a debate on the question: "Ought the Georgia Guard to be continued in the Cherokee Nation?" The nays won nine to three.

Governor Gilmer noted that no other official act brought him more abuse than imprisoning the missionaries. "The subject excited great interest throughout the country," he said, and brought "mortification" to the people of Georgia.[2]

As serious as the issue was for the nation, something more explosive took the highest priority for President Jackson: the union of the United States was in jeopardy.

South Carolina, after angrily protesting trade tariffs (taxes on the purchase of overseas goods), now openly discussed nullification. Jackson's Vice-President, John C. Calhoun, elected on a separate ticket, articulated the South Carolinian belief that the Constitution could not be greater than its creators, the sovereign states. If a federal law threatened the sovereign state's existence, then South Carolina could justifiably "nullify" that law or secede from the Union. Because tariffs on manufactured goods forced southerners to buy the North's manufactures at a higher price, they believed the Yankee tariff laws were grossly unfair.

Jackson, although a Southerner, was an adamant defender of the Union and warned against the foolish talk of nullification. The positioning came to a climax on April 13, 1830, at an annual dinner to celebrate the birth of Thomas Jefferson. Jackson rose to make a toast and glared at his Vice-President across the table: "Our Federal Union—it must be preserved!"

Calhoun was reported to have slightly spilled his yellow wine, his hands trembling. After a few minutes Calhoun rose and made a toast: "The Union," he declared. "After our liberty, the most dear!"[3]

Jackson believed in a strong federal government and promised to use force on South Carolina if she wavered. But if the Supreme Court ruled in favor of Worcester, the President would find himself facing the expectation of enforcing federal laws against another Southern state as well—Georgia. Such an action might cause them to join the rebellion with South Carolina, which he knew he could keep under control if she remained in isolation. To accomplish that, Jackson needed to be rid of the missionary problem.[4]

It was in relation to this crisis that Ann Worcester was told one day that her husband was changing his mind in prison. The news came from a man named Dr. David A. Reese who had traveled to the area to visit his distant cousin. Ann demanded that the man explain himself. Reese said he had gotten the news from an unimpeachable source—Governor Gilmer of Georgia.

Ann did not know that Reese had been sent as a plant to discreetly spread news that might dishearten the Cherokees. Neither did Samuel Worcester know that a friendly visitor from Athens, Georgia—who traveled to the Millidgeville prison just to see the missionaries—was also an agent of the Governor.

Dr. Alonzo Church, president of Athens University, was a Vermonter by birth, like Worcester. The distinguished scholar genuinely complimented the two prisoners for their unswerving devotion to their principles. He insisted on spending money to provide comforts for them in their cells.

Eventually, he asked them if they had given careful thought to the possible ramifications of their actions. Did they realize that forcing Georgia to obey a Supreme Court case against her will could lead to civil war?

Worcester told him that such a thing wouldn't happen if men like him counseled Georgia's leaders to do the proper thing. And on that note, their first conversation ended. But a seed was planted.[5]

John Ridge and cousin Elias traveled north during the months of waiting for the Supreme Court's decision. The *Commercial Advertiser* praised John for his speech in New York: "[He] is rather tall and slender in his person, erect, with a profusion of black hair, a shade less swarthy, and with less prominence of cheekbones than our western Indians. His voice is full and melodious, his elocution fluent, and without the least observable tincture of foreign accent."

John spoke with some of the same style that made his father the most celebrated orator in the nation: "You asked us to throw off the hunter and warrior state: we did so," he said. "You asked us to form a republican government: we did so—adopting your own as a model. You asked us to cultivate the earth and learn the mechanic arts: we did so. You asked us to learn to read: we did so. You asked us to cast away our idols and worship your God: we did so."[6]

A large amount of money was collected after the convincing talk. In Philadelphia, the cousins spoke again. John gave another excellent, rational speech. But Elias was more emotional this time. He expressed his grave concerns over the President's refusal to intercede in Georgia's oppression. Emotion was understandable, but this time his tone bordered on hysteria. Perhaps he had the foresight to see future events. Perhaps he was drawing from Jackson's recent statement after vetoing the central bank legislation. The President said, "The executive is not bound by the decision of the Supreme Court."

"What shall we do?" Elias had cried to the crowd. "We are distressed," he shouted.

"We are distressed!"[7]

Chapter Sixteen:

The Reversal

In the days of waiting for a Supreme Court decision in *Worcester v. the State of Georgia*, the two missionaries had spent over six months in prison.

Letters from friends were common. Little Turtle, a student, wrote to Dr. Butler: "I'm not afraid of what the Georgians are doing," he said, "for you have done no wrong."

Butler had a young wife and a newborn. The children from his deceased wife wrote letters beginning, "Dear Pa."

Worcester no longer had the advantage of receiving letters from his great mentor, Jeremiah Evarts, who had died in the weeks past. "By standing firm in this case and being willing to suffer for righteousness sake, you will do much to encourage the Cherokees," Evarts had written his disciple on the eve of the incarceration.

In fact, Evarts seemed to think the entire Cherokee Nation was in the balance regarding this crisis: "Courage is the one thing they want. Long courage or fortitude; it is the very point, in my judgment, where they will lose their country and their earthly all," he said.

Evarts did not believe the Cherokees should face the fire alone: "Now God is likely to bring this trial upon white men of a select character who went out for a holy purpose; that is, to give their labor and their lives, if need be, to the Cherokees."

Evarts was no longer alive when Dr. Church made his second visit to the Milledgeville Penitentiary to discuss the broad issues of the case with Samuel Worcester. The specifics of the discussion are not recorded, but he reported to the Governor that he had found Worcester "less fiercely convinced."[1]

If the ruling powers could convince Worcester to change his mind, no Supreme Court decision would be necessary. Governor Gilmer was more than willing to extend a pardon.

The Moravian mission board instructed their missionaries to leave the state. The Methodist missionaries, likewise, had been severely censured for meddling in politics. The denomination expressed official regret for the earthly actions of its missionaries. But they assured the Cherokees of their "unabating zeal for the conversion and salvation of their souls."

Butrick continued to be an opponent, and had developed somewhat of a rivalry with Worcester after the board sided with the imprisoned missionary. Ann Worcester pleaded with Rev. Butrick to take "the larger view,' but, according to his journal, Butrick had even threatened to resign from the American Foreign Mission Board. He himself had managed to escape imprisonment—what he called "the mad dog,"—by residing in Tennessee and itinerating to Georgia for mission work.

When the Supreme Court's decision was announced, John Ridge and Elias Boudinot were in Boston at the offices of the American Mission Board, the Calvinistic group of Congregationalists and Presbyterians that now were alone in their political stance. A friend arrived from Washington and asked them if they were prepared to hear the worst.

No, they were not, Ridge replied.

Then the friend brought the good news. The Court had ruled that the imprisonment of Worcester was unconstitutional, along with all the laws regarding the Cherokees that Georgia had enacted.

"The Cherokee Nation, then," John Marshall's decision said, "is a distinct community, occupying its own territory . . . in which the laws of Georgia have no right to enter but with the assent of the Cherokees."

"The Act of the state of Georgia . . . is consequently void."

The celebrants there with the cousins, ironically, were board members Lyman Beecher—who earlier had banned Elias from Cornwall—and John Pickering, the Indian linguist whose devices were snubbed by Worcester for Sequoyah's.

Boudinot asked Dr. Beecher if he'd heard the news.

"No, what is it?" And when Elias explained, Beecher jumped up and clapped his hands. "God be praised," he shouted and ran off to tell his family.[2]

In the Cherokee Nation, the news reached back into the farthest coves. They held "frolics" to celebrate the great victory over Georgia. Many who had enrolled with emigrating agents for the West, reversed their decision.

John Marshall's fellow justice, Joseph Story, was relieved to be part of the 5-4 majority: "The court can wash their hands clean of the iniquity of oppressing the Indians," he said.

Historian Marion Starkey captured the jubilation just after the decision with this remark: "No saint of legend had ever been more spectacularly vindicated by sundry miracles such as the turning of bread into roses. This was the best kind of miracle, evidence that man would render justice to man, that the ideals of the republic had not been empty words."[3]

It was in this ideal of the American republic that the Ridges, Elias, John Ross, and the entire Cherokee Nation had placed their lives, their trust and hope. The destiny of their people depended on it. Without that commitment to the rule of law in America, all their plans and strategies as a people collapsed. Without it, they may indeed be annihilated and become extinct, as had many tribes before them.

And perhaps that was part of the reason for Elias's unusual and highly emotional speech in Philadelphia. There had been some speculation that President Jackson may not enforce the decision of the Supreme Court, even if they did rule in favor of the Cherokees.

Such speculation was too horrible to entertain, the ramifications too terrible to consider. But it took only a few days after the March 3, 1832, decision before John Ridge started hearing reports that Jackson may do that very thing—defy the Supreme Court despite the fact that such defiance would create a constitutional crisis.

In early April, John Ridge prepared for a meeting with the President to directly confront him on the reports. Before the meeting he had written a letter with much bravado, calling Jackson a "chicken snake." We will cut off the chicken snake's head, he said, not allowing him time "to crawl and hide in the luxuriant grass of his nefarious hypocrisy."

But while John Ridge was one of the greatest statesmen the Native Americans ever produced, he was no match for one of the most fearless fighters and ruthless negotiators in all of American history. It was nearly impossible to stare down Jackson in a face-to-face meeting.

Jackson informed him directly and clearly that he would not enforce Marshall's decision. Secondhand reports say the President remarked, "John Marshall has made his ruling, now let him enforce it." It would not have been out of character for him to make such a statement. When the news first reached Jackson, documented history shows he told John Coffee: "The decision of the Supreme Court has fell still born."[4]

Jackson explained the meaning of this to John Ridge— that he had received no papers from the Court yet to enforce anything. For that to happen, the Supreme Court must receive in writing from the Georgia courts their refusal to release the prisoners. And the prisoners themselves must issue a writ to the Supreme Court, who in turn must inform the President to take action.

Jackson pointed out that the Court had already adjourned and would not reconvene until January, eight months away. And even when they did, Jackson was confident that the Georgia court would not send up an official letter. Federal law had no provision for curing such a problem, he told Ridge.*

Jackson may have been bluffing in part. Certainly he seemed to think he had the authority to correct South Carolina's insolence. But he was correct that, by letter of the law, he would not be required to publicly make a decision on the missionaries for another eight months—not until Worcester and Butler sent an official writ to the Court asking for relief.

Whatever Ridge felt about the constitutional soundness of Jackson's arguments, he apparently became fully convinced of the President's intention to refuse enforcement of the Worcester case, whatever the rationale might be. The Cherokees' idealistic belief in the United States' commitment to the Rule of Law—since the Treaty of 1794 with Washington—perished in the view of John Ridge at that moment. For the first time in his life he considered the possibility that removal may be the Cherokees' only option.

---

*On Jackson's supposed statement: "John Marshall made his decision, now let him enforce it," Remini says, "Jackson said no such thing. It certainly sounds like him, but he did not say it because there was nothing for him to enforce. Why . . . would he refuse what no one asked him to do? Why would he make such a foolish remark? Rather, he said that, 'The decision of the Supreme Court has fell still born, and they find that they cannot coerce Georgia to yield its mandate.'" (Robert V. Remini, *Andrew Jackson and His Indian Wars*, p. 257.)

He must have reacted visibly in front of the President. Jackson wrote to Coffee that day: "I believe Ridge has expressed despair—that it is better for them to treat and move."

"Ridge left the President with the melancholy feeling that he had heard the truth," wrote cabinet member Amos Kendall. "From that moment he was convinced that the only alternative to save his people from moral and physical death was to make the best terms they could with the government, and remove out of the limits of the states."[5]

Such an immediate reversal seems unbelievable, and it may not have happened as quickly as Kendall reported. But undoubtedly Jackson delivered the key blows to Ridge's confidence in that meeting. He stared into John's eyes in the same way he stared down Russell Bean on the frontier and forced him to drop his guns.

Jackson's biographer, Robert Remini, describes those eyes: "They instantly registered whatever emotion or passion surged within the man. And seeing them ignite signaled anyone in close range to run for cover. Indians came to appreciate what that signal meant. They said he merely had to look at them that way and they dropped lifeless to the ground."[6]

If John had lost hope for the legal system in his heart, he officially and on the record continued to express optimism.

Anything less would have been too much for the Cherokee people to digest in the current crisis. By the time the council met in July, John had already convinced his father and cousin Elias that Jackson and the United States would never protect them in the East. But the council as a whole, led by the ever-hopeful Principal Chief John Ross, was not persuaded. The proceedings were kept secret from the public, and the Cherokee Nation officially told Washington they expected their rights to be enforced as defined by the Supreme Court. And they expected to see Worcester and Butler released.

The eyes of the entire nation were now on two missionaries in a prison in rural Georgia. The Cherokees themselves believed the prisoner's efforts would somehow sway public opinion into forcing Jackson's hand. Evarts' warning to his friend Samuel Worcester now seemed prescient: "If you leave, I fear the Cherokees will make no stand whatever."

Despite Jackson's confident front with John Ridge that he would never be faced with enforcing the Supreme Court's decision, he now became obsessed, behind the scenes, with schemes to make sure he was never confronted with the possibility. Up to this point he had said nothing publicly on the matter. And he would never need to if the missionaries were persuaded against sending up a writ to the Supreme Court.

This was crucial for the President, because the controversy with South Carolina was now erupting. Congress passed Jackson's new tariff bill in July. Now, Calhoun's home state promised to leave the Union over the oppressive and unfair tax.

Jackson also faced reelection in November. Opponents criticized his duplicity regarding federal authority over states rights. The National Republicans called the President "the persecutor of the missionaries and the Indians—and the destroyer of the independence and authority of the judicial branch of the government."

The *Boston Daily Advertiser* accused Jackson of treating the "ministers of Christian religion with open outrage. He loads them with chains; drags them from their peaceful homes to prison; commits them in defiance of law like common criminals to the Penitentiary, and violently keeps them there, against the decision of the highest law authority."[7]

The American Mission Board wrote to Jackson directly, asking him to release their missionaries. The President continued to avoid public statements on the controversial matter, providing only a vague response with this side comment: "I cannot refrain from observing that here, as in most other countries, they are by their injudicious zeal (to give it no harsher name) too apt to make themselves obnoxious to those among whom they are located."

Despite these controversies, Jackson was reelected in early November, winning states in every part of the country.

It did not take South Carolina long to respond. On November 24, 1832, a convention called by the state legislature passed the Ordinance of Nullification. Federal agents were ordered to stop collecting customs duties after February 1. If Jackson used force to collect the taxes, South Carolina would immediately secede, the convention declared.

John C. Calhoun rode north to resign as Vice-President. Jackson now faced the worst constitutional crisis since the founding of the country.

The President promised to use force to quell the rebellion, but feared that Georgia and other states might join. This meant disaster. So all efforts were placed on convincing the missionaries to give up. Inconveniently, these heavenly minded prisoners did not respond to arguments of force, so other strategies were implemented.

Governor Gilmer invited Ann Worcester and Lucy Butler to the Governor's mansion for dinner. Over a candlelit feast he provided gentle and rational arguments for why their husbands could now go home and keep their integrity. The women said they would leave the decision to their husbands.[8]

Worcester received a letter from "a lover of my God and country" who lived in Washington. The writer also argued that they could honorably ask for a pardon. The Court had exonerated them. But their current intransigence would either cause the Supreme Court to lose its authority or cause the nation to erupt in civil war.

"There is a growing inclination to believe that you are agents for the purpose of producing political effects," he wrote. "You may not be so generally considered martyrs if things come to the worst."

The scholarly friend from Athens, Dr. Church, continued his visits and seemed to be making progress with the missionaries. Whereas Worcester and the Board had formerly called Georgia's actions "something that should never be expected from a Christian people," Worcester now had a different tone toward these Southern Christians: "They are exceedingly sensitive and great care must be taken not to touch roughly any sensitive strings," he wrote to Boston. "There may be much piety and fear of the Lord even with those who support measures which, at a distance, it would seem as if piety and the fear of the Lord would utterly preclude."[9]

On November 26, two days after South Carolina's convention, the missionaries instructed their attorneys to send their writ to the Supreme Court, which was scheduled to reconvene in January.

But the never-ending arguments and gentle persuasions still bothered Worcester. Now his conscience was tormented by the idea of causing a breakup of the Union. Worcester had been a patriot since his youth, when at the age of eighteen he wrote a poem about his beloved country:

> And thou Columbia? The happy seat
> Where Liberty and Science kindly meet;
> Whose laws, with easy yoke and gentle rein,
> The strength, and beauty of the state maintain.[10]

He had much time to wrestle with his thoughts. He pondered his early idealism that produced such poems. And he certainly thought of the many sermons he had preached, including the one most often cited in his journal from this text: "What shall it profit a man if he gains the whole world, yet loses his own soul?" There was also the sermon that John Ridge translated for him on Psalm 1: "The wicked are like chaff that the wind blows away."

But the wicked had not departed so easily in this situation. Worcester had been in prison over a year now, and might spend another three years away from his wife and children. "It would require the military force of the United States to effect our release," he later wrote. "And if [Jackson] did, it would not benefit the Cherokees."

The Constitution ought to be tested, he determined, "when a man of different principles should be at the helm of government." The current man at the helm wasn't being blown away by the wind, it seemed.[11]

On December 7, the missionaries wrote to Boston, asking the board's opinion on whether they should remain. On Christmas Day, the board members held an emergency meeting in their offices at Pemberton Square. Southern critics of New England and its zealous missionaries often pointed out that it was easy for them to oppose removal—they had driven out their Indians a century before. They might have a different view if the issue affected their soil. Now it did.

Over the objections of Evarts' successor, David Greene, the American Mission Board voted in favor of instructing the missionaries to give up.[12]

The day the letter arrived, the two prisoners wrote Governor Gilmer. They withdrew their suit, lest it "might be attended with consequences injurious to our beloved country."[13]

Two days later, Jackson, no longer worried that Georgia would join in a rebellion, presented Congress with his Force Bill.

His opponents blinked. On January 21, South Carolina suspended nullification.

Dr. Elizur Butler

Stand Watie

CHAPTER SEVENTEEN

THE COLLAPSE

Principal Chief John Ross was greatly disappointed by a letter he received from the American Mission Board in Boston—written two days after their letter to Worcester—that urged the chief to make a treaty for removal.

Jackson's Indian Removal Bill did not in fact give him power to forcibly remove them. What it did was legally determine that the area was in the jurisdiction of the states. It also added Congress's stamp of approval to removal treaties that in the past had been negotiated solely by the President. The Cherokees' survival was bleak apart from being ruled by their own laws, and removal seemed all but inevitable. But Jackson still needed a treaty with the chiefs to obtain his goal—to move them swiftly to the West.

Publicly, Ross did not condemn the American Mission Board in Boston—he only called the decision "premature." And he certainly could not criticize the two missionaries who had sacrificed more than anyone could have expected as individuals. But Ross now was convinced that the Cherokees no longer had any allies in white America.

He had called for a day of prayer and fasting several months before, after the Ridge delegation returned and was convinced that the legal system no longer provided any hope.

Ross insisted that the deliberations of the past summer be kept private. The council also decided to suspend the Constitution—only in effect now for four years—and forgo national elections during the crisis. He also blocked Boudinot from printing anything in the *Phoenix* sympathetic to removal. A free press no longer existed in the Cherokee Nation.

Perhaps Ross felt he must retaliate in kind—that if Jackson could ignore his Constitution, the Cherokees could move to a state of martial law. But his high-handed actions only further alienated him from John Ridge, who had hoped to be elected Principal Chief himself. Bitter factionalism emerged between the Ross party and the Ridge party.

Ross believed he was acting to save his people from Jackson's schemes: "The object of the President . . . is too plain to be misunderstood," he said. "It is to create divisions among ourselves, break down our government, our press and treasury, that our cries may not be heard abroad."[1]

Ross and Jackson were actually much alike. They both were of Scottish descent. They were wily, tough, determined, and both obsessed with protecting the vital interests of their respective peoples.

But whereas Jackson's patriotism was developed on his own, Ross's stemmed from a long line of Cherokee advocates. His great-grandfather, William Shorey, was one of the first white men to master the native language. His grandfather John McDonald, who married Shorey's half-blood daughter, hailed from Inverness, Scotland, and as Britain's Indian agent served as the first white man in the entire area. Dragging Canoe himself joined McDonald at his trading post on Chickamauga Creek near Lookout Mountain and set up his military headquarters there until the warriors were crushed in 1792. McDonald was Dragging Canoe's chief advisor.

Ross's father Daniel Ross, also a Scot, married McDonald's daughter and built a house at the foot of Lookout Mountain where young John was raised as a backwoods aristocrat. John later moved to an area two miles south (now known as the town of Rossville) into a house built by his grandfather—McDonald had since sold his first cabin and farm to the Brainerd Mission in 1817.[2]

Eventually, Ross built another large home and plantation fifty miles down the road at the Head of Coosa (now

Rome, Georgia), conveniently next to the complex of Major Ridge, twenty years his senior. The two often met for discussions in each other's homes.

Ironically, many were now accusing the Ridges of being Indians who thought like the whites, whereas Ross was always viewed as a chief with white blood who thought like a red man. He never backed down from Andrew Jackson. That determination would forever haunt Jackson's legacy.

But the arguments now coming from the Ridge party could not be ignored by the Principal Chief. John Ridge noted that Cherokees were being robbed and whipped daily by Georgia authorities. Worcester said a murder seemed to occur every few days.

"Fortunate drawers" were now claiming their prizes in the Georgia lottery, which included the plantations of all the chiefs in the nation. To complicate matters, Georgia officials determined that Shadrach Bogan, the lottery commissioner, had surreptitiously rigged the lottery wheel so that five of his friends obtained the best prizes. One of them was the house and 160 acres owned by John Ridge.

Lottery winners were not yet supposed to occupy the properties, and Dr. Butler, encouraged by Ross, continued to fight in the courts for his Cherokee friends who were being pushed off their properties. But then the settlers moved into Butler's mission church, took his horses, and began peering into his home while his young wife and children slept. He eventually moved across the line into Tennessee. His parishioners wept.

Ross himself came home one day to see his plantation seized and his wife and children sequestered into two small rooms of the house. He too had to move to a log cabin in Red Clay, Tennessee.[3]

The Ridge party argued that they could not survive under state jurisdiction. They would be crushed by racial oppression. Moving west would save them from total annihilation. Never would the terms be more generous than the present for removal.

"I know you are capable of acting the part of a statesman in this trying crisis of our affairs," John Ridge wrote to Ross in the midst of their growing rivalry. "After all, we know upon consultation in council that we can't be a nation here. I hope we shall attempt to establish ourselves somewhere else. Where, the wisdom of the nation must try to find."

He may have been referring to places south, not west. John Ross at one point held secret negotiations with agents of Mexico and of Texas—still an independent republic—to see if terms of removal in those nations might be acceptable. His grandfather had conducted similar talks for

Dragging Canoe with Spain. But Ross's plans never materialized.[4]

Even the Principal Chief's brother, Andrew Ross, traveled separately to Washington and signed a removal treaty—one that fell on deaf ears and that even the Ridges opposed due to its paltry terms.

In fact, John Ross himself did eventually conduct removal negotiations with Washington after the exasperated Ridges sent their own delegation without the approval of council. Ross asked for $20 million, almost the amount of the entire national debt.

"Filibuster!" Jackson said in defiance and flatly refused the offer. Ross shot back with an offer to take any amount decided upon by the Senate, a suggestion Jackson immediately accepted, to Ross's surprise.

When the upper body agreed to an amount of $5 million, Ross withdrew his offer.[5]

Ross managed to keep these unpopular negotiations under wraps when the council met again in August. The Ridges believed they were acting more forthrightly. Boudinot had resigned as editor of the *Phoenix* long before, after Ross prevented him from expressing his views. "I love my country," Boudinot said, "I cannot tell them we will be reinstated in our rights when I have no such hope."

Ross said that diversified views at this point would only cause confusion and injure the nation: "The love of our country demands unity of sentiment and action for the good of all."

Boudinot resigned without acrimony: "I have done what I could," he said diplomatically. "I have served my country, I hope with fidelity."

But when Boudinot and the Ridges spoke at the next council, they found themselves enjoying very little popular support. Boudinot said he had reached the "unpleasant and most disagreeable conclusion" that their lands were about to be taken. "Now, as a friend of my people, I cannot say 'peace, peace' when there is no peace," he said.[6]

Tom Foreman, a sheriff for the nation, rose to speak. He accused Major Ridge of being an enemy of the people. While he was addressing the council, someone in the audience said, "Let's kill them!"

A stunned John Ridge defended his father's honor and reminded them of his long service to the nation. Major Ridge, who was tired and who now deferred public speaking duties to his son and nephew, rose to address the crowd. He said the sun of his existence was going down and he had only a short time to live.

"Where are your laws! The seats of your judges are over-turned. When I look upon you all, I hear you laugh at me," he said sadly. "I feel on your account oppressed with sorrow. I mourn over your calamity."

A petition to impeach the Ridges, with 144 signatures, was then presented. But Ross eventually blocked the measure. On the last day of council, news arrived regarding the fate of John Walker, another Cherokee who had taken it upon himself to treat separately with officials in Washington. He was dropped from his saddle by the bullets of assassins hidden behind a log. The Ridges went home by a different route to avoid the same fate.

Andrew Jackson received the news of Walker's assassination while at his home in Nashville, Tennessee. He was incensed. He sent word demanding the killers be prosecuted. But they never were found.

Major Ridge told John Ross about rumors of a man named Thomas Woodward who had been given word by the Principal Chief to have him assassinated. Ross denied the charge adamantly: "It is high time all such mischievous tales should be silenced," he said.

Ross's calls for peace did not stop the violence. A Ridge party man named Hammer was beaten until he died. A man named Crow—asked to officiate a frolic while others drank and danced—was stabbed sixteen times. Two followers of the Ridges named Murphy and Duck were also stabbed to death at another frolic.

There were also rumors of the Ridge party plotting to assassinate Ross: "Partyism should be discarded," insisted the Principal Chief. "Our country and our people—should be our motto."[7]

Both sides made attempts to get beyond partisanship. While Ross kept the Ridges from being impeached, John Ridge fought for Ross when he was arrested. The Georgia Guards claimed that Ross, a slave owner himself, was working to instigate a riot among the slave population of Georgia. His papers were also seized. There was no truth to the allegations, and John Ridge, who was now on more favorable terms with Georgia officials, talked with them for three hours. They let Ross go.

Eventually, representatives of both parties met and reached an agreement to send a delegation of twenty leaders to negotiate a possible removal treaty. When, in John Ridge's perception, that agreement was broken, he spoke out bitterly against Ross.

"Ross has failed," he said, "before the Senate, before the Secretary of War and before the President. He tried hard to cheat you and his people, but he has been prevented. In a day or two he goes home no doubt to tell lies."

At this point, the Ridge party determined to take matters into their own hands, despite the threats to their safety. It was now common for them to see men surrounding their homes in the evening, wrapped to their eyes in blankets, sending a menacing message of danger.

They met with Jackson's agent at New Echota to sign their own treaty apart from Ross. They had tried all they could to work with the Principal Chief, said Boudinot: "It was not until that hope was eradicated by your continued evasive and non-commital policy," he told Ross, "that John Ridge broke his connection with you, to do the best the times and circumstances permitted."[8]

Seventeen chiefs signed the Treaty of New Echota, including Major Ridge, John Ridge, Andrew Ross, Elias Boudinot, and his brother Stand Watie. But less than 100 came to the meeting that John Ross implored the Cherokees not to attend.

Boudinot asked where the others were, like Tom Foreman and his cohorts, who had threatened them once before in council.

"Ross has induced them not to come," he said. "They will come again. I know I take my life in my hand, as our fathers have also done. We will make and sign this treaty. Our friends can then cross the great river, but Tom Foreman and his people will put us across the dread river of death! We can die, but the great Cherokee Nation will be saved."[9]

New Echota was named after the old town of Chota, the city of refuge for those who feared the avenger of blood under the old tribal laws. But these Cherokee leaders suffered no illusion that they would escape death.

Neither did Elias's beloved wife, the former Harriet Gold, escape death in New Echota. Not long after her husband signed the treaty, she grew deathly ill after her seventh child, a son, died in childbirth.

"She suffered extreme bodily pain throughout her whole sickness," said Elias. "She complained of darkness in the fore part of [her mind], but towards the latter, she said the darkness was removed, that there was a clear sky between her and her Redeemer."

The morning before she died, she called to her husband while in great bodily pain. "The is the last night I shall spend in this world," she told him. "Then how sweet will be the Conqueror's song." She was buried in a small cemetery at New Echota.[10]

To John Ridge and his father, New Echota also meant their deaths. They both said they had signed their death warrants upon signing the Treaty of New Echota.

Just before attaching his mark to the document, Major Ridge also rose to speak to the small crowd about his ancient homeland: "I know the Indians have an older title," he said. "We obtained the land from the living God above. They got their title from the British. Yet they are strong and we are weak. We are few, they are many. We cannot remain here in safety and comfort. I know we love the graves of our fathers . . . but an unbending, iron necessity tells us we must leave them."

Again he spoke: "I would willingly die to preserve them. But any forcible effort to keep them will cost us our lands, our lives, and the lives of our children. There is but one road to safety, one road to future existence as a Nation. That path is open before you. Make a treaty of cession. Give up these lands and go over beyond the great Father of Waters."[11]

Those assembled voted seventy-six in favor, seven against.

The agreement's terms included an exchange of lands in the West and $5 million for the Cherokee treasury to help with removal and to establish the nation in the Arkansas territory.

Jackson finally obtained the document he needed. Despite its absurdly small numbers—and a petition from the Ross party with almost 16,000 signatures* (nearly the entire Cherokee population)—he convinced the senators that it represented the will of the Cherokee people. John Quincy Adams spoke out against the fraudulent treaty, calling it an "eternal disgrace upon the country."[12] The Senate ratified the Treaty of New Echota by a margin of one vote on May 18, 1836.

Jackson urged all members of the Cherokee Nation to begin their journey to the West. All who did not voluntarily leave would be forcibly removed by federal troops within two years.

Almost the entire nation defied his warning.

---

*The figure is in dispute. Robert Remini, in his book *Andrew Jackson and His Indian Wars*, cites 12,000. Thurman Wilkins (*Cherokee Tragedy*, p. 292) comments: "Many [were] duplicated and many fraudulent—even suckling babies were found to have 'signed' the petition. With all the questionable names, however, the protest represented a formidable opposition among the Cherokee people."

CHAPTER EIGHTEEN

THE TEARS

O n May 23, 1828, soldiers began entering the homes of the Cherokee people. As many as 8,000 souls were gathered in the first roundup.

"Families at dinner were startled by the sudden gleam of bayonets in the doorway and rose up to be driven with blows and oaths along the trail that led to the stockade," wrote ethnologist James Mooney, who interviewed hundreds of those who participated in the march to the West. "Men were seized in their fields or going along the road, women were taken from their wheels and children from their play."

Historian Marion Starkey said the people captured were of every type: "There were men and women so old and gnarled that they seemed more like supernatural beings than human flesh. There were newborn babies. There were the blind; until that moment the missionaries had no idea that there were so many blind in the Nation. There were dying consumptives who had to be carried on litters.

"There were the devout. Epenetus was picked up on the road when he was returning from helping Butrick administer the sacrament at Brainerd, and he was not allowed to return there to fetch his young son, but was thrust into a keelboat on the Tennessee and shipped all the way to Arkansas without having a chance to find out what would become of his boy.

"Sometimes when the soldiers came battering at the doors, gentlefolk said, 'Let us pray first.' Then the soldiers stood sheepishly by while a man fitted spectacles over his nose, got out a queer little book printed in Sequoyah's characters, and read from it to his family."

The white settlers waited just behind the soldiers—"like vultures," wrote General John Ellis Wool, who later asked to be relieved of his agonizing post. "[They] are watching, ready to pounce upon their prey and strip them of everything they have."

"Sometimes the Cherokees were interrupted when they tried to gather possessions in a blanket, and were ordered to leave everything as it was," wrote Starkey. "Arrangements would be made later. Sometimes sales were made on the spot. . . . Beef creatures, rocking chairs, cherrywood tables, castiron kettles, fiddle saws, homespun blankets, and patchwork quilts went for a twelfth of their value or for nothing at all. One Cherokee recalled that his cabin had been made the scene of an impromptu auction; very distinctly he recalled the price fetched for his blue-edged plates, twenty-five cents apiece. But who got the money? The auctioneer perhaps? Anyway, he never saw it."[1]

Many of their ancestors' sacred graves were also immediately plundered, and silver objects and medallions taken as treasure.

The prisoners were taken to eleven stockades located in a forty-square-mile area that centered around Ross's Landing at the Tennessee River next to Lookout Mountain. These concentration camps proved to be as deadly as the long march itself. Little provision was made for waste, and the Indians were forced to sleep on the cold ground. Soldiers gazed at the women who had no walls to hide themselves.

"They were obliged to live very much like brute animals," wrote Daniel Butrick in his journal of the Trail of Tears that is still published today. "And during their travels, were obliged at night to lie down on the naked ground, in the open air, exposed to wind and rain, and herd together, men, women and children, like droves of hogs, and in this way, many are hastening to a premature grave."

"We understand that four died in the camps yesterday," he wrote on August 7, "making the number of deaths at that place twelve in thirty-six hours."

Dr. Butler identified a fatal sickness he called "putrid dysentery." He reported seventeen deaths in one camp in one week of this cause alone. By October, he estimated that 2,000 had died in the camps.

Butrick said soldiers would roam around the camps at night near Brainerd "endeavoring to find Cherokee women and girls." Missionary Vail saw six soldiers at Ross's Landing surround two Cherokee women by a tree and try to get them to drink whiskey. He reported it, but later the soldiers had the women out all night.

Another married woman was caught by soldiers and "either through fear or other cause was induced to drink and yield to their seduction, so that now she is an outcast, even in the view of her own relatives. [Who knows] how many of the poor captive women are thus debauched."

The estimated 14,000 exiles were divided into groups of about 1,000. Some were loaded into keelboats for the first leg of the journey, and some were marched on foot the entire way. Around 2,000 left in the two years before, heeding the warnings of the Treaty Party, but the first section of the forced removal embarked on September 1. Butrick reported that on that day the Chickamauga Creek next to Brainerd Mission was lower than anyone living had ever seen it.

Many parties marched across the Cumberland Plateau to Nashville, then Hopkinsville, Kentucky, then to Golconda where they crossed the Ohio River, and then west to cross the Mississippi near Jonesville. From there they marched southwest through the Arkansas territory and, finally, to what is today called Oklahoma.

Chief White Path, who had so fervently questioned the wisdom of modeling the white man's Constitution, died on the Trail. So did John Ross's full-blood wife Quatie, who gave her blanket to a shivering child, who ultimately lived. Most of the infants died, as did a majority of those over sixty.

Butrick reported the plight of one pregnant woman who barely made it across the Tennessee River from Ross's Landing, and then fell on the riverbank. "A soldier coming up, stabbed her with his bayonet, which, together with other pains, soon caused her death."

Another man refused to march any longer, saying he had gone as far toward the Arkansas as he should ever go. "He loaded his rifle, lay down at the foot of a tree, with his rifle by his side, the muzzle toward his head, and by means of his toe, discharged his gun, and thus put an end to his existence."

"Upwards of a thousand Indians passed by today," wrote an eyewitness to the long march. "The scene seemed like to me more like a distemporal dream or something from the Dark Ages than like a present reality, but it was too true."[2]

Despite their horrible fate, many of the Cherokees themselves clung to their faith. "We were rejoiced to hear the praises of God, in Cherokee," Butrick wrote, "ascending from so many places at the same time, yet without confusion."

Dr. Butler estimated that 4,000 died on the trail, but later upped his estimate to 4,600. On March 25, the last group arrived in "Arkansas." Dr. Butler, who had preached from Lamentations just before embarking on the journey, delivered a general funeral sermon to honor all those who died along the way.

One member of the Georgia Guard who later served in the Confederate Army described the horror of the removal: "I fought through the Civil War and have seen men shot to pieces and slaughtered by thousands, but the Cherokee removal was the cruelest thing I ever saw."

"This history of the Cherokee removal," said James Mooney, "may well exceed in weight of grief and pathos any other passage in American history. It became known as "the trail where they cried."[3]

CHAPTER NINETEEN

THE AVENGER

When the last group of Cherokees finally arrived in the new territory, Dr. Butler wrote to a colleague in Boston to describe the tragedy. He also described the rage: "All the suffering and all the difficulties of the Cherokee people were charged to the accounts of Messrs. Ridge and Boudinot," he sadly reported.

John Ridge's son, John Rollin, later gave his opinion of the real scapegoat: "The ignorant Indians, unable to vent their rage on the Whites, turned their wrath towards their own chiefs."

John Ridge was not afraid to place some of the blame on Ross for the deaths and the loss of property: "If Ross had told them the truth in time, they would have sold off their furniture, their horses, their cattle, hogs and sheep."[1]

John and his father and cousin left voluntarily several months beforehand, and were already busy with building new homes. John believed the people he talked to were all happy with their new homeland in the Ozark Mountains, which sharply resembled the lush forests and streams of Appalachia.

Boudinot was working with Worcester on translating the Gospel of John. The missionary, however, was confronted by both the Ross settlers and the old settlers who had arrived years before with their disapproval of his alliance with Boudinot. Worcester had to fight with the authorities to keep Elias at the mission, and the lingering enmity left Worcester with a foreboding concern.

The people knew that the cousins had met with Andrew Jackson at the Hermitage, his Nashville mansion, on their way to the Arkansas. The Cherokees' confusion was compounded by the fact that John named his newest son Andrew Jackson Ridge. In the minds of the people, those powerful blue eyes had apparently mesmerized Jackson's former sworn opponent into some kind of sad delusion. Biographer Thurman Wilkins gives this explanation:

"The reversal of John Ridge had the pattern and much of the intensity of a religious conversion. First had come doubts, suppressed into the depths of his being, and then the reintensification of old beliefs. There had followed the shock of newly perceived reality, in this case the apprehension of what must surely be the fate of his people if they should remain in their old domain under existing conditions—the inevitable degradation, even destruction. . . . In his childhood his parents had dedicated him to the service of his people, an understanding he had never evaded, no matter how strong his personal ambition. What mattered most was the Cherokee people, a consideration always at the back of his mind; they could not be allowed to perish. Suddenly, at the critical moment, came the shift of his whole mental organization, swift and total, forever changing his outlook. As soon as Ridge had renounced the cause of antiremoval, he espoused the cause of emigration with equal fervor, with what might even be called fanaticism." [2]

New political challenges emerged when the new settlers, led by Ross, met in council with old settlers, who, like Sequoyah in 1821, had emigrated west years before. The Treaty Party leaders hoped that perhaps the talk of violence would lessen as the two bodies reached unity. But the talks initially were stormy, and when the Ridges were seen talking with leaders of the old settlers, the anger of New Echota blazed forth once again. There was more talk of assassination in accordance with the Blood Law that had been reaffirmed by the Treaty Leaders in 1829.

Late in the evening of June 21, a secret meeting was held at which the Blood Law was read along with the names of the signers of the New Echota Treaty who were scheduled to be executed: Major Ridge, John Ridge, Elias Boudinot, Stand Watie, John A. Bell, James Starr, and

George Adair. The conspirators succeeded with some of those named, but not with all of them.

Those present were instructed to draw from a hat, and twelve of the men drew an *X*, which assigned them to the deed of execution.

In the early hours of the next morning, those assigned to Major Ridge followed the chief as he returned from a trip to Cincinnati, Arkansas, a few miles from his son John's home at Honey Creek. They hid behind brush in a place overlooking the likely place for a traveler to cross White Rock Creek.

Major Ridge stopped on a large flat rock next to the stream and allowed his horse to rest and take a drink. Several rifles crackled with fire. Major Ridge slumped in his saddle and fell from his horse, his head and body riddled with five bullets. A boy accompanying him rode off to tell the terrible news to John, but a courier sent by Sarah Ridge intercepted him.

About this same time, not coincidently, a band of thirty men waited in the woods just out of sight of the home that Elias Boudinot was building for his family. (He had since remarried a missionary, Miss Delight Sergeant.) He spent the night with Worcester's family a mile away. As he walked to the building site, where several carpenters were at work, four Cherokees approached him to ask for medicine—a normal request as Boudinot was currently in charge of distributing the public medicines.

As he walked back toward the mission house, two of them dropped behind him. One then plunged a knife into his back, and he screamed and fell into the grass. The other man then swung a tomahawk into his head and split it open. He swung the weapon several more times until the head of Elias Boudinot, once known as Buck Watie, was gashed in six or seven places.

The carpenters, hearing the shriek, ran to help, but the others had already fled. His wife rushed to Elias as he was dying, but his eyes glazed over just as she called out his name. Worcester rushed to the scene immediately. "They have cut off my right hand!" he cried.[3]

A few miles away at Honey Creek, twenty-five men surrounded the home of John Ridge. Three quietly entered the house with their rifles. The sister and brother-in-law of Sarah Ridge, who left her family in Cornwall to join the Cherokees, slept unharmed in another bedroom. The three crept silently into John Ridge's bedroom while he slept. One man pointed at his head and pulled the trigger. It failed to fire.

Chaos ensued. The eyewitness account of the event was written years later by John Rollin Ridge, who was only twelve when he watched men drag away his father:

"Our family was aroused from sleep by a violent noise. The doors were broken down, and the house was full of armed men. I saw my father in the hands of assassins.

"He endeavored to speak to them, but they shouted and drowned his voice, for they were instructed not to listen to him for a moment, for fear they would be persuaded not to kill him.

"They dragged him into the yard, and prepared to murder him. Two men held him by the arms, and others by the body, while another stabbed him deliberately with a [knife] twenty-nine times. My mother rushed out to the door, but they pushed her back with guns into the house, and prevented her egress until their act was finished, when they left the place quietly.

"My father fell to the earth, but did not immediately expire. My mother ran out to him. He raised himself on his elbow and tried to speak, but the blood flowed into his mouth and prevented him. In a few moments more he died, without speaking that last word which he wished to say."

After the twenty-sixth wound, the men threw Ridge high into the air. When his bleeding body fell to the ground, each one stamped on the body as they marched over it in single file.[4] John Rollin continues:

"Then succeeded a scene of agony the sight of which might make one regret that the human race had ever been created. It has darkened my mind with an eternal shadow. In a room prepared for the purpose, lay pale in death the man whose voice had been listened to with awe and admiration in the councils of his Nation, and whose fame had passed to the remotest of the United States—the blood oozing through his winding sheet, and falling drop by drop on the floor.

"By his side, my mother, with hands clasped, and in speechless agony—she who had given him her heart in the days of her youth and beauty, left the home of her parents, and followed the husband of her choice to a wild and distant land. And bending over him was his own afflicted mother, with her long, white hair flung loose over her bosom, crying to the Great Spirit to sustain her in that dreadful hour.

"And in addition to all these, the wife, the mother and the little children, who scarcely knew their loss, were the dark faces of those who had been the murdered man's friends, and, possibly, some who had been privy to the assassination, who had come to smile over the scene."

Sarah Ridge sent a courier to warn her father-in-law of the pending danger. But he returned after meeting up with the boy who accompanied Major Ridge.

The boy delivered the news to Sarah and to John's mother. Major Ridge was dead.

Elias Boudinot's wife sent a friend immediately to her brother-in-law, Stand Watie, to warn him of the assassins. He received the message in hush tones in a store that was occupied by followers of the Ross party.

Watie hurried out back and jumped on Worcester's horse, Comet, whose name stemmed from her reputation for speed.

Watie escaped the killers. But, according to a story that Wilkins says may be legend, he returned later in the evening to view his slain brother's body. He stepped into the house amid the throng of people that included Ross partisans.

He drew back the sheet, took a long look at the disfigured face, and turned to the crowd. He promised $10,000 for the names of those who murdered his brother.[5]

John Ross failed to offer up any names to the federal government, claiming he had no knowledge of the plot. But Watie blamed him for the assassinations, and roamed the countryside with fifteen accomplices to kill the murderers. Ross was forced to retain armed guards.

When the council met again, the old and new settlers were able to reach an agreement. They also offered amnesty for all crimes since the removal, in effect acquitting the killers of Watie's kin. Many considered the killings lawful executions, but the three Cherokee leaders never were allowed a trial by jury as required by the 1829 Blood Law. And neither did the killers ever face one.

That same council offered amnesty to any signers of the Treaty of New Echota if they came forward and confessed their wrongdoing. Seven did so. But Watie and John Bell refused, defiantly replying that they would rather die than accept such humiliating terms.

In 1842, Watie killed James Foreman, one of the alleged murderers of the Ridge, as well as several other accused assassins. At one point, Ross had as many as 500 bodyguards. More of the Ridge party were also killed. The Cherokee territory turned into a land of chaos and revenge that rivaled any blood feud of old.

President James K. Polk urged Ross to divide the country. Facing such a measure, Ross reluctantly called for a meeting, and the two factions agreed to a truce in 1846.[6]

After 15 years of relative peace, the nation was divided again over a war between the states that Worcester—who died in 1859 while still serving his people—thought he had prevented by accepting a pardon from prison.

Two decades later, the Dawes Commission broke up much of the Cherokee Council's title to the land and portioned it off to individual Cherokees. As leaders like the Ridges predicted if such a scheme was allowed in the East, the individual landowners sold it quickly or lost it through fraud or exorbitant taxes. By the turn of the century, less than ten percent of the land given in the Treaty of New Echota was owned by Cherokees.[7]

Other large portions of Cherokee land were divided into 160-acre tracts by the federal government. Thousands of settlers in 1893 lined up with horse and wagon and waited for the starting gun to fire before rushing in to claim the best tracts of the Cherokee Strip. These Oklahoma "Sooners," romanticized today in the movies, in large part sold their properties again and headed further west until Manifest Destiny was finally stopped by the Pacific Ocean.

EPILOGUE
WHO BETRAYED THE CHEROKEES?

Though over 200,000 now claim Cherokee citizenship, most of them have never heard of Major Ridge, John Ridge, or Elias Boudinot.

Of the two figures most recognized, one is Chief John Ross. They know he led them across the wilderness in the Trail of Tears.

Ross died in 1866 in Philadelphia, where he stayed after being captured by the Union following his help in bringing the Cherokee Nation into the Confederacy. The Union commander told Lincoln that Ross had tried as long as possible to keep the nation neutral, and recommended the Principal Chief be treated as an ally.

The other historical figure most recognized by modern Cherokees is Stand Watie. He never wavered in his devotion to the Confederacy, ultimately earning the rank of Brigadier General, the only Indian to reach such a high level on either side. Even today, he is revered as the last Confederate general to surrender.

Watie never forgot his brother's murder, and the Ridge and Ross factions remained bitter opponents for decades. The feud has largely disappeared today, perhaps echoing modern man's forgetfulness of most history.

But students of the events of the early 1830s soon learn that the questions between Ridge and Ross continue. To some degree the question will always be a mystery: Did removal save the Cherokees from extinction?

Related to that question is an issue of justice: Were the Treaty signers murdered or were they justly executed? And did John Ross have any knowledge of the conspiracy? That, too, remains an enigma to this day.

A century and a half of reflection has provided a bit more consensus on some of the questions, but historians still hold strong and differing views regarding who deserves the blame for the tragedies.

THE RIDGE PARTY

Noted author Paul Johnson dedicates two pages to the Cherokee saga in his popular *History of the American People*. The removal took place because "a greedy minority led by Chief Major Ridge" signed a treaty with Jackson, he writes.[1]

His offhand remark reflects 150 years of misinformed popular sentiment regarding the cause of the Treaty and the removal. Perhaps a simple bribe is easier to comprehend than the complex nature of the contest or the unthinkable injustices of the day.

When Worcester preached the funeral sermon over his slain friend Elias Boudinot, he praised his "loveliness, integrity and Christian worth." The only event of his life, he told his listeners, that could even be considered questionable, was his signing of the Treaty.

But no serious Cherokee historian believes that bribes motivated Boudinot or the Ridges. "Years of diligent search [showed] not the slightest taint of dishonesty in the lives of Stand Watie, Boudinot, or the Ridges," wrote Grant Foreman, a preeminent Cherokee historian, in his *History of Oklahoma*. "Indeed, there is no proof," says Thurman Wilkins, author of *Cherokee Tragedy*.

Neither do these scholars believe the counterpoint charges that Ross was motivated financially. Jackson, who called the slight Ross that "little villain," always believed financial gain was the reason behind his intransigence, accusing the principal chief of opposing removal to retain his position and property. Indeed, several of his relatives prospered from his help, including brother Lewis who became the richest man in the nation—unfortunate for John Ross's reputation says author Ethan Allen Hitchcock, "though it is fair to consider that this may have resulted from contracts properly made."[2]

Personal ambition has been identified as a reason for the actions of John Ridge, who hoped to be elected Principal Chief. But most conclude that he knew when he signed the Treaty that he was destroying future ambitions. He said it himself, speaking in third person: "You say John Ridge was prompted by a selfish ambition when he signed that treaty. It is not so. John Ridge signed his death warrant when he signed that treaty. . . . Sooner or later he will yield his life as the penalty for signing.

"Let it not be said that John Ridge acted from motives of ambition, for he acted for what he believed to be the best interests of his people."

So the remaining question is not one of integrity but one of judgment. Did the Ridge party act in the best interests of their people? Did they help the Cherokees?

John Ross told the Ridge party that if the Cherokees remove west they will encounter "no other prospect than the degradation, dispersion and ultimate extinction of our race."[3]

Ross's prediction did not come about. The Cherokee Nation survives today. But in what form?

"The kind of nation that the Cherokees became in the West was far different from what they had worked so hard to be in the East," concludes William McLoughlin in *Cherokee Renascence in the New Republic*. "It lacked that simple, buoyant idealism and hope . . . as equals in the future destiny of the republic that had inspired them prior to 1833.

"This is not to say that the Cherokee people or their culture died," McLoughlin notes. "The Cherokees are more numerous today than ever. And cultures do not die; they simply develop in new ways."

But many cultures have indeed died, notes the biographer of Andrew Jackson.

"Despite the obscene treatment accorded to the Cherokees by the government, the tribe not only survived but endured," writes Robert Remini in *Andrew Jackson and His Indian Wars*. "As Jackson predicted, they escaped the fate of many extinct eastern tribes. Cherokees today have their tribal identity, a living language, and at least three governmental bodies to provide for their needs. Would that the Yamasees, Mohegans, Pequots, Delawares, Narragansetts, and other such tribes could say the same."[4]

The curator of the Cherokee Heritage Center, the Nation's official museum, says the Ridge and Ross feud still lingers. "The Treaty Party didn't get any money, but a lot of people still think that," said Sam Watts Kidd in an interview with the author.

Ms. Watts Kidd believes Ross would be perceived today as the "betrayer" if he had been successful when he traveled to Washington to meet for a treaty: "That tells me that if the price was right, he would have sold it."

"I try to see both sides," she said, "but when you get right down to it, I probably would be more pro-treaty."

She said she came to the Heritage Center years ago "thinking the Ridges and Elias were traitors. But I've pretty much changed my mind."

"If John Ross had just set there—if no treaty were signed—then there would be no Cherokee Nation today."[5]

There is little doubt that the Ridge Party knew of their fate in signing the treaty. "I expect to die for it," said Major Ridge.

"If I can relieve my bleeding countrymen," said John Ridge, "I am even prepared to be immolated to gratify the ambitions of my enemies."[6]

There is also little doubt that the Ridge party leaders believed they were doing the right thing. The Ridge himself, who "Walked Along the Tops of the Mountains," was given that name in part because the people believed he could see far into the distance from his lofty position.

Perhaps he could.

John Ross

Whereas history has been generally kind to the long-time Principal Chief of the Cherokee Nation, not everyone believes he is without blame for the suffering of his people.

There were, of course, a large number of Cherokees more stubborn than Ross and those who joined him on the Trail of Tears. These patriots ran from the federal soldiers and hid in the mountains. Many died, but hundreds more survived and were later gathered together in their own mountaintop country—a remarkable story for another book. That place is now Cherokee, North Carolina, home of the sovereign nation of the Eastern Band of Cherokees.

"In the eyes of this group, Ross's final capitulation made him no less a traitor than Ridge," writes historian Marion Starkey in *The Cherokee Nation*. "It is the descendants of these who today keep alive the confused tradition that Ross was Jackson's man and plotted with him to achieve the abomination of removal."

While that theory is not tenable, many believe that Ross could have averted much of the bloodshed.

"[Ross] shares a portion of blame for this unspeakable tragedy," writes Remini. "He continued his defiance even after the deadline for removal had passed. He encouraged his people to keep up their resistance, despite every sign that no appreciable help would be forthcoming from the American people or anyone else; and he watched as they suffered the awful consequences of his intransigence."[7]

Curator Watts Kidd agrees: "A lot of the tears and death could have been prevented. The people should have been more informed," she said. "I think that's when the tides turned—when John Ross denied Elias Boudinot the ability to print the truth of what was exactly going on."

There are also some, especially descendants of the Ridge party, who believe Ross betrayed the Cherokee Nation by allowing its greatest and most talented leaders to be murdered.

Others continue to believe the killings were legal. "Avarice and greed of both the white man and a few Cherokee tribal members expedited our removal," writes the editor of the *Cherokee Observer On-Line*. "The illegal signing of the removal treaty resulted in the deaths of the signers; Major Ridge, John Ridge, Elias Boudinot, and others were executed under the Cherokee 'Blood Law.' Their deaths were justified, according to Cherokee law."

The Blood Law itself, which all three victims signed, spelled out clearly the process: the accused must appear before the Cherokee Nation's Supreme Court. Yes, the law allowed for the outlaws to be chased down and killed, but only if they "shall refuse, by resistance, to appear at the place designated for trial."[8]

Major Ridge, John Ridge, and Elias Boudinot did not run from a trial and were never tried for their offense. And it is still difficult to ascertain whether John Ross had any knowledge of the plot or whether he ever knew the names of the killers in order to bring them to justice.

Wilson Lumpkin, Georgia governor during the removal, was bitter against Ross.

"The best half of the intelligence, virtue and patriotism of the Cherokee people has been basely murdered, to gratify the revenge and ambition of John Ross. And it remains a crying sin against the United States that the murderers of the Ridges and Boudinot have not been punished as justice and law demanded," he wrote. "The righteous blood of these Abels will yet cry for vengeance."[9]

On the other hand, Worcester, no Ross partisan, believed the Principal Chief was the sole force for keeping the Ridge members alive during the three years before the removal. A Moravian missionary reports secondhand that when Ross received the news of the killings, he said, "Once I saved Ridge at Red Clay, and would have done so again had I known of the plot."[10]

But suspicion of Ross's complicity remains today: "To say John Ross didn't know anything about it is ridiculous," says Watts Kidd.

Clearly, the descendants of John Ross knew it was an Achilles heel for the longtime Principal Chief. A document at the Gilcrease Institute in Tulsa provides a typescript testimony of Ross's son, Allen Ross, given on Christmas Day in 1891 before his death a few months later. He said he made the statement at the request of his two grandsons. Several historians quote from it in evaluating John Ross's involvement.

"I know that my father did not know anything about this matter," the statement says.

A secret meeting was held, he said, "without the knowledge or consent of my father John Ross." In that meeting, names were drawn from a hat to determine the assassins for each signer. But the chairman told Ross's son to stay with his father that night "to keep him from finding out what was being done."

The next day they went to visit a friend, and some men passed by and threw something in the yard. "My father asked what it was. I told him that it was a stick. I afterwards returned and found that it was the knife which is still in my possession. These men were some of the full-bloods who had participated in the killing of Mr. Boudinot a few minutes before."

"I know that my father did not know anything about this matter."

Then written in typescript at the end: "(Signed) Allen Ross."

Further investigation only compounds the historical enigma. The document in the Gilcrease special collections shows that the statement is in fact not signed by Allen Ross. Instead, there is a handwritten note in pencil at the end by W. W. Ross, who says his father Allen Ross died on April 21, 1891.

"I was present at the time of his death. He told me this knife was one used in killing of Boudinot." W. W. Ross gave the knife to the Oklahoma Historical Society. His handwritten addendum is not dated.[11]

Apart from a conclusion on that particular matter, this author believes that John Ross can be viewed as a hero, as can Major Ridge, John Ridge, and Elias Boudinot. And this remains true even if one concludes the Ridge Party deserved execution and even if Ross was complicit in those killings. Both parties may have saved their people—one saving their physical existence and the other preserving the memory of their greatness.

Whereas many Cherokees, including the revered Sequoyah, left their homeland decades before, these great men led their people with poise, sacrifice, and great wisdom and erudition for two decades. They stood side by side with strength, courage, and unity. Their accomplishments are enormous. But the enemy proved to be overwhelming. Eventually they all collapsed, some later than others, under the pressure and the great injustice that was backed by overwhelming force. They were successfully turned against each other.

When confronted with such horrible circumstances, even the best of men can crumble.

Others may argue that the greatest heroes are the likes of Dragging Canoe and Tecumseh, who never trusted the white man and continued to push for armed resistance.[*]

Many historians agree that Ross was a great leader because he acted as the people wanted. The Cherokee

---

[*]Eerily, Tecumseh's prophecy to the disagreeable Creeks and Cherokees—when he said that at his arrival in Detroit he would stomp his foot upon the ground "and shake every house in Tookabatcha"—seems to have been fulfilled. Three weeks later, about the time it took to travel to Michigan, a violent earthquake hit the land of the Creeks and severely damaged Tookabatcha. Indians who had counted the days it would take for Tecumseh to arrive home ran outside as houses collapsed and shouted, "Tecumseh has got to Detroit! Tecumseh has got to Detroit! We feel the shake of his foot!" The divine nature of his prophecy was strengthened by the sudden arrival of a comet—Tecumseh also predicted that his arm of fire would stretch across the sky. (H. S. Halbert and T. H. Ball, *The Creek War of 1813-1814*, pp. 79–80.)

people did not want to leave their ancient homeland, and they were willing to suffer greatly to demonstrate their resolve. Ross is to be commended for his sensitivity to the popular will and perhaps his sense that a demonstration of civil disobedience was necessary for such a horrible injustice to be remembered in history.

As the exhibit on the Trail of Tears reads at the Cherokee Heritage Center: "This event has become a symbol for the suffering of all Indian people."

THE MISSIONARIES

On December 13, 1833, the Cherokees awoke to a dazzling meteor shower across the sky that lasted for several hours. "The world was literally striped with fire," wrote the editor of the *Phoenix*, who chose to leave the cause to the astronomers.

But for weeks, the people speculated on the meaning of the heavenly sign, and many chose to see ominous events ahead.

Indeed, the nation fell into immediate decline and became bitterly divided in the months following the sign from heaven. Months before the meteors hit, the missionary board had made its ominous decision that they would no longer oppose the political agenda of removal.

Starkey believes Worcester continued to struggle with doubt about his decision for several years. Only two months after accepting a pardon, he was informed by Boudinot that the South Carolina nullification and secession threat had been resolved.

"Without war?" asked Worcester.

"Oh," he said, "they aren't going to war, much less for the Indians."

Perhaps, in fact, he would not have caused a war had he remained in prison. The only reason Worcester had given up was to prevent one.

Others speculate, conversely, that a civil war initiated by Worcester in 1833 might have been a much shorter conflict and would have been much easier for the North to win. The tremendous bloodshed of the 1860s might have been avoided.

McLoughlin says it would have made no difference if the two missionaries had stayed put and forced a response to Marshall's decree. "Jackson would have found reasons to refuse and voters would have supported him."[12]

Later in his career, Worcester found favor with the Ross faction and labored in building the largest mission in Indian territory, and the first co-ed educational institution west of the Mississippi. But the early years were difficult.

He wrote to his brother-in-law to refute rumors that he had advised his close friend Boudinot to sign the treaty, a rumor purportedly coming from his cellmate, Dr. Butler.

"So far from having ever given any such advice, I have always distinctly and decidedly exercised my disapprobation of such a course," he insisted in an 1839 letter, just months before the assassinations. The statement was heavily underlined. He also assumed that Butler's statement had been misconstrued.

A few years before, he and Butler experienced a small divide when the doctor followed Ross's advice over Worcester's and chose to fight in court to retain the mission property being taken by Georgians. He also decided to stay in Red Clay, Tennessee, rather than remove early to Arkansas like Worcester. Ultimately, Butler joined the large contingent of Cherokees who crossed in the forced removal.

So did missionary Butrick, who over time became a staunch Ross supporter and continued his vocal opposition to the Treaty leaders and his personal rivalry with Worcester. The American Mission Board warned him against partisanship, an ironic switch from his earlier disparagement of political involvement by missionaries.

Two years after the American Mission Board reversed its position on removal, Butrick conducted the ceremony of the Lord's Supper in the old country. Precisely during the time of the communion service, a full solar eclipse took place. Butrick provided a scientific explanation.

"It sounded reasonable," writes Starkey, "but some of his parishioners saw no harm in getting an opinion on possible deeper meanings of the event from a more ancient source. In Cherokee lore Sun was closely related to Ancient Red, the Grandparent Fire. Sun-Fire was the only proper recipient of prayer. For this reason some converts had the confused impression that Sun-Fire was what Butrick meant by God. Now they had seen that God sicken nearly to death before their eyes while they broke the bread and drank the wine which were God's own body and blood."[13]

Indeed, some Cherokees believed the Christian God had failed them. Whereas the missionaries successfully brought the message of salvation to many individual Cherokees—and today churches abound in the nation— they were not able to save the Cherokees' homeland.

It would be unfair to say the missionaries betrayed the Cherokees. Arguably, some of them were great heroes. But neither can they be given credit for redeeming Cherokee culture.

Andrew Jackson

To this day, there are Indians who will not carry a twenty dollar-bill.

Cherokees know they like John Ross and Stand Watie. And they also know who they don't like: Andrew Jackson.

During his eight years as President he signed over seventy treaties and provided over 100 million acres of Indian land to the states to gratify their settlers.

The beliefs undergirding his actions are best articulated in his December 3, 1833, speech following reelection. Regarding the two tribes holding out, the Seminoles and Cherokees, he said: "They have neither the intelligence, industry, the moral habits, nor the desire of improvement which are essential to any favorable change in their condition. Established in the midst of another and superior race and without appreciating the causes of their inferiority or seeking to control them, they must necessarily yield to the force of circumstances and ere long disappear."

Some conscientious historians seek to distinguish between genetic and ethnocentric racism. Jackson held the latter, they say. He believed the Indians had the ability to improve but remained inferior because they chose not to improve. But, as McLoughlin reports, the genetic argument was growing in Jackson's day and "the two positions were slowly shading into each other."[14]

Jackson's presidential opponent, Henry Clay, may not have been much better, and arguably may have been worse. In his diary, John Quincy Adams said Clay thought full-blooded Indians as a race "were not worth preserving. He considered them as essentially inferior to the Anglo-Saxon race which were now taking their place on the continent. . . . Their disappearance from the human family would be no great loss to the world."[15]

Remini, Jackson's biographer, agrees that this man called "Sharp Knife" by the Indians deserves some of the blame for the Trail of Tears, but not all.

"Andrew Jackson has been saddled with a considerable portion of the blame for the horror of removal. He makes an easy mark. But the criticism is unfair if it distorts the role he actually played. His objective was not the destruction of Indian life and culture. Quite the contrary. He believed that removal was the Indian's only salvation against certain extinction.

"The Indian problem posed a terrible dilemma," Remini writes. "He could have imitated his predecessors and done nothing. But that was not Andrew Jackson."

As hard and cruel as the policy was, many of Jackson's contemporaries believed it to be kind and necessary. "Indeed, many historians today agree with that conclusion," notes Remini. He mentions author Paul Prucha, who provides "a very convincing argument supporting Jackson's actions." Likewise, Paul Johnson says hindsight "proves Jackson was absolutely right. A series of independent Indian republics in the midst of the United States would, by the end of the 20th century, have turned America into chaos."[16]

Jackson was a man of his day. "Like most Americans at the time, he was a racist (not that he had the faintest idea what that meant)," writes Remini. "But he was not a madman intent on genocide. Removal was meant to prevent annihilation, not cause it."

But he notes that Jackson and his fellow Americans may may have betrayed something else: "They understood the rationale behind removal and approved it," said Remini. "What they and Andrew Jackson failed to realize was that they had betrayed some of their most cherished ideas about American justice and decency."

Nevertheless, to the day of his death, Jackson believed he acted in the Cherokees' best interests. "I have no motive, Brothers, to deceive you," he often said. "I am sincerely desirous to promote your welfare."

Jackson scholars generally agree that national security and the preservation of the republic were Old Hickory's primary motivators, not racism. His treatment of the Indians proceeded from that agenda.

Just before he died on June 8, 1845, he wrote to a friend: "I am now like Simeon of old; having seen my country safe, I am prepared to depart in peace."[17]

"He left believing he had saved the Indians from inevitable doom," wrote Remini in 1990. "And, considering the tribes which have survived to this day, perhaps he had."

But after ten more years of focused study on the subject, the Jackson scholar removed all doubt for himself. He believed Jackson rescued the Cherokees from annihilation: "Although that statement sounds monstrous, and although no one in the modern world wishes to accept it or believe it, that is exactly what he did."[18]

For Jackson's modern critics, Remini is quick to point out that Andrew Jackson's actions were backed by great popular support. A majority of Americans "applauded the President's action in settling the Indian problem once and for all."

Jackson and his followers argued that they saved the Cherokees from annihilation. They certainly persuaded the Ridges such was the case. But for those who take that position, the paradox remains that Jackson was the very one most responsible for creating the Cherokees' problem. After three decades of empowering settlers to overpower the Cherokees and their lands, Jackson then attempted to play the role of the hero. He did save them from a situation that may have destroyed them. But he was largely responsible for creating the situation. And while the Ridges may have been wise enough to see the only path left for survival, they should have also had the sense to form only a cautious alliance. Wisdom and discretion suggests against befriending and fraternizing with such a longtime, ruthless enemy.

McLoughlin places the larger blame on the popular spirit of the time: "Who can say precisely why the Age of Reason with its faith that all men are created equal gave way between 1789 and 1833 to the Age of Romanticism with its conviction that the United States was 'a white man's country'?"

When Alex de Tocqueville toured the U.S. during the 1830s, the famous Frenchman wrote glowing reviews on the greatness of the American experiment. He is still quoted today. But de Tocqueville also criticized the nation regarding its treatment of Indians.

He captured the irony: "It is impossible to destroy men with more respect for the laws of humanity."[19]

America is a nation led by those elected by the people. In that light, Andrew Jackson was not the ultimate party responsible for betraying the Cherokees. We betrayed the Cherokees.

AUTHOR'S POSTSCRIPT

REMEMBERING THE BETRAYAL

The countryside looks very similar. That was my first observation as I drove from my hometown in Chattanooga into Tahlequah, Oklahoma, to interview the Principal Chief of the Cherokee Nation.

The foothills of the Ozarks bear a striking resemblance to the mountains and streams of East Tennessee and North Georgia.

You must pass through Arkansas before reaching Tahlequah. A few minutes from the Oklahoma line I found the site of Major Ridge's assassination, thanks to the help of a descendent of John Bell, a fellow Treaty signer. The Arkansas site remains unmarked, behind barbed wire.

The Ridge's body was initially buried nearby. It was not moved next to his son at the Polson Cemetery in Honey Creek, Oklahoma, until 100 years later. At that time, John's tomb was also unmarked. But in 1930, a marker was placed on the graves of both son and father in the Polson cemetery.[1] Only basic information is provided on the granite tablets, along with a mention that John was assassinated nearby.

Stand Watie is also buried in the remote family-owned cemetery, and a lengthy tribute is inscribed on a large marker to his honor.

About 200 yards past the graveyard sits a quaint white farmhouse owned by John Ridge's third great-granddaughter, Nancy Polson Brown. She grew up with stories from her grandfather, who also cared for the graves. Now Nancy's sons, Matt, twenty-two, and Ridge, twenty, cut the grass and pull weeds around the humble tombstones.

Nancy says John Ridge's daughter Flora married a Dr. Polson and he ended up owning the Ridge property.

"My grandfather showed me the area where the house was," she told me in an interview. "John Ridge's funeral was held at night. I heard the reason the graves weren't marked for so long was because they might be desecrated."

She said she has a relative in Minneapolis who told her he owned the shirt John was wearing when he was killed. She wrote him once in the 1970s for more information, but the letter was returned.

Apparently, there are no more descendents with the last name of Ridge. But at least thirty-five Ridge progeny met for a reunion last year (August 2002) at the restored home of Sarah Ridge in Fayetteville. Sarah moved her family to that Arkansas town to avoid danger after the killings. A drama troop performed a reenactment for the gathering.

While the Ridge and Ross feud is mostly over, people still have strong opinions. Some of her relatives still don't care greatly for John Ross. "It's still in the back of your mind," said Nancy.

She does believe the Ridges spared the Cherokees from extinction. "I think it would have worked out better if John Ross would have prepared them to move," she said.[2]

As you drive from Honey Creek to Tahlequah, it is difficult to find evidence of a traditional culture. There is no reservation. The roads, schools, and buildings are first rate. Churches abound. Even the Wal-Mart looks just like ours in Chattanooga except for the fact that half or more of the shoppers are clearly Native American.

The Tahlequah Chamber of Commerce Visitor Center looks like any city's welcome center, with brochures on all the local attractions, including a few old homes and museums. They give away American flags there. The Lord's Prayer in Sequoyan hangs in a frame on the wall.

The attendant there told me he is 1/64 Cherokee. He'd never heard of the Ridges. He did know that John Ross was a chief who brought them across the Trail of Tears.

You can't find traditional Cherokee food anywhere in the area, even though the Principal Chief's complex is fronted by an eatery called The Restaurant of the Cherokees.

The sign written in chalk says Today's Buffet is fried chicken, hamburger steak, and sauerkraut.

A young waitress, one-third Cherokee, told me customers don't say much, but one angry couple left after seeing the menu. "What did they expect," she asked with a Generation X tone, "corn soup and mutton?"

She did note that they served traditional Cherokee fried bread. "It's not what grandma made, but it's pretty right on."

Neither did Principal Chief Chad Smith, one-half Cherokee, provide any visible Indian giveaways. (He did tell me they were quite comfortable with the word "Indian.") His modern office and sharp dress were upstaged by his articulate responses to questions for my book. He has an M.B.A. and a law degree, and the

University of Georgia graduate coached me on several aspects of the 1830s—a decade I had been studying for over two years. He noted ironically that when he lived in Georgia as a student, he was deemed an incompetent witness if he were ever called to testify. The banning of Indian witnesses was still on the books.

"The 1830 treaty gave the United States the authority to exchange lands," he told me. But instead the Cherokees became victims of simple racism. Their land was "basically taken by official extortion," he said.

Of the fifteen million acres in the West the Cherokees were given in the Treaty of New Echota, Chief Smith said Cherokees own only one-third of one percent of those holdings today. Against the will of the tribal council, the land was distributed in the late nineteenth century to individual Cherokees. Smith says ninety percent of tribal lands were gone within fifteen years through "selling off, fraud, or to pay taxes."

Even today, there are efforts to seize their remaining lands. "There's actually a group in Oklahoma called One Nation," said Chief Smith. "Their desire is to 'level the playing field with the tribes,' fearful that our gaming and authority over water and air quality management creates an unlevel playing field. This basically comes from the oil and gas industry that was successful in taking the oil and gas reserves and tearing up the surface interests—abandoned mines, abandoned oil fields and such."

Chief Smith says the arguments used by big oil and big tobacco are the same ones used by Georgia in the 1830s—that a sovereign tribe can't exist within a sovereign state. "We hear that argument today, 'How can there be another sovereign in the state of Oklahoma?' You go to Congress, you hear it.

"We find there is a long history, that if we have assets, non-Indians want those assets.

"Our political institutions were more sophisticated than Georgia and Tennessee. We were ninety percent literate, which was probably ten times the rate of Whites in those surrounding states. We passed a Constitution—that's what galled Georgia, that we had a constitutional government within its borders.

"Look at the Navahos. Nobody wanted those territories, but when you find uranium there, you find an effort to take it over. And that's what happened in North Georgia and Tennessee. When you actually look at what happened after the tribes moved, a few folks made some money off of it and left it as a wasteland.

"Eighty percent of the settlers alienated their lands within fifteen years because they weren't of the quality or quantity to sustain themselves. Basically, the economics of North Georgia was not farming. The Cherokees used it very well in a subsistence economy—hunting and fishing and such. But if you go now to North Georgia, it's sparsely populated. Western North Carolina is sparsely populated. It's only now with the urban sprawl of Atlanta and maybe Chattanooga that there's been any significant population.

"So there was sufficient territory for 14,000 folks to have survived, but it just wasn't politically popular."

So what now? Should white America apologize or should there be reparations for past injustices?

"If you'd live up to the initial agreements, we'd be happy," he said.

Like politicians in D.C. who fret over students who've never heard of Cornwallis or Yorktown, Chief Smith sees the need for modern Cherokees to learn their history. He says they've all heard of the Trail of Tears. But they may know little else.

Over 2,400 have now graduated from a forty-hour course on Cherokee heritage taught by a Ph.D. from New Mexico.

"Instead of trying to right the wrongs of the past, or many times trying to fight the oppressive ignorance of the country, we focus on trying to improve our own quality of life," he said, "which we think we can achieve by just continually visiting our own language, our own culture, our own stories. To some degree, these are things of the past. We see them as stories of inspiration rather than stories of desperation."

Asked about the actions of the New Echota Treaty signers, Chief Smith believes their course of action made sense to them.

"What they envisioned at the time was rational," he said. "Where history refuses to pardon them is the arrogance of saying their analysis was superior to the vast majority of the Cherokees."[3]

The Chief believes the Ross and Ridge faction still existed thirty years ago, but no longer. However, even twenty years ago, evidence of the feud emerged when two statues were unveiled simultaneously outside the Cherokee Heritage Center, the nation's primary museum located in the woods about five minutes from Chief Smith's building. Just past the entrance sits a small church, the Jesus Christ Church of Eternal Jubilee—Full Gospel.

The Heritage Center was established on the site of the Park Hill Mission founded by Samuel Worcester. Only a few large pillars exist following a fire that destroyed the major landmark. You walk past them as you enter the Center's front door.

I talked with one of the workers behind the counter, a forty-year-old full-blood. She spoke perfect English. She grew up Baptist, she said. She can't speak Cherokee, but can understand the language. I asked if she was familiar with John Ross, John Ridge, or Elias Boudinot. She had only heard of John Ross, but didn't really know anything about him.

Indeed, just outside stand five statues honoring great Cherokees. The only two from before the twentieth century are John Ross and Elias Boudinot. They are both wearing suit and tie. They were created by the same artist who sculpted the Iwo Jima statue. Ross and Boudinot were unveiled at the same time in 1983.

"Still, there's a lot of animosity about it," the center's archivist told me.

Ross's memorial states that he served as Principal Chief from 1828–1866. "Loyal to the Cherokee People thru five decades of public service," it says. Ross is quoted: "I am an old man, and have served my people over fifty years. And now I look back, not one act of my public life rises up to abraid me. My heart approves of all I have done."

Elias Boudinot's statue identifies him as editor of the *Cherokee Phoenix*, as clerk of the Cherokee National Council, and as a signer of the Treaty of New Echota. "True to his convictions through all adversity," the memorial states.

He is quoted as well, from his famous speech in Philadelphia: "I can view my native country, rising from the ashes of her degradation, wearing her purified and beautiful garments, and taking her seat with the nations of the earth."

He is also quoted from his somber speech as he signed the Treaty of New Echota: "Oh, what is a man who will not dare to die for his people? Who is there here who will not perish if this great nation may be saved?"

Both Ross and Boudinot are buried about a mile and a half from the Center. Small signs point clearly to the Ross cemetery. You go a mile past and take a left. The famous Principal Chief's grave lies among the more numerous small tombstones outside the special gated section reserved for his brothers and family members. Apparently, Ross chose to be associated with the populace, even in death.

You take a right to get to Boudinot's grave. There is a cemetery farther down on the right side of the road. But that's not it. Boudinot's cemetery is not really marked.

No signs from the road will get you there. But as you drive past the other cemetery, when you look back you can see a small fenced area on the other side of the road that was blocked initially by the woods. Opening an unlocked gate lets you drive a couple of hundred yards on grass to a quiet pasture with a few trees.

To the right sits about ten or twelve tombstones. Four are outside the low fence. Above one of those is a large marker in honor of Elias Boudinot—assassinated by enemy tribesmen, it says. Literature on the gate says Boudinot was buried on the Park Hill Mission property right where he was assassinated, "his grave covered by a large slab of stone with no inscription."

Later, it was identified as Boudinot's and marked. But Curator Sam Watts Kidd believes Boudinot's actual grave sits next to it, underneath a pile of large rocks.

Inside the fence—placed there later by relatives—are the graves of Samuel and Ann Worcester and their off-spring. Ann died in 1840 in childbirth, just after Boudinot's death.

Samuel's stone says the following: "For 31 years a missionary of the ABCFM serving the CHEROKEES. To his work they owe their Bible and Hymn Book."

Upon Worcester's death, according to the information on the gate, the American Mission Board closed the mission, saying they believed the Cherokees "were no longer a heathen people."

The information also describes decades of neglect of this cemetery. Livestock wandered through and broke headstones. But interest revived in the 1950s and the plot was then deeded to the Oklahoma Historical Society.

On the trip back to Chattanooga—sort of a reverse route of the Trail of Tears—I rode with a woman whose grandmother was a full-blood. I saw her old Bible, in the Sequoyan translation.

My travel companion's husband was the principal of a Cherokee school for three decades. They still call their football team the Stillwell Indians. Students have names like Hummingbird, Pumpkin, Buzzard, Fourkiller, Mankiller, and Wolf.

"They don't know anything except what's written in the history books," she told me. But they do still cling to a good bit of conjuring and old Indian "superstition." But she said they never talk about it in front of white people.

My residence back in Chattanooga is located, appropriately, about five blocks from Ross's Landing, the launching pad to the Tennessee River that became the epicenter for the start of the Trail of Tears.

A month before, 100,000 bikers had made their annual September trek called "The Trail of Tears," in which they commemorate the Cherokee tragedy by following the route of the historic long march.

One biker told me it is the largest cavalcade of motorcyclists in history. "The motorcycle parade was to span 200 miles, beginning in Chattanooga along the Tennessee River," reported the *London Independent* regarding the event that now draws international attention. "The trek has been called one of the defining moments in native American history," added the British paper.[4]

The landmark aquarium built next to Ross's Landing commemorates the Trail of Tears with inscriptions on the stones outside—including quotes from Dragging Canoe, Ross, Jackson, and the Cherokee Constitution.

A statue of a pre-contact native stands across the street by the river. Simply entitled "Cherokee," it was a gift from one prominent Chattanooga family to another. The town fathers of Ross's Landing met in a small log cabin in the summer of 1838 to name the new city they had acquired from the Cherokees—at the same time the

Indians were being gathered in camps less than a mile away for the removal.

After several names were nominated, including Lookout City and Albion, they chose the Indian name "Chattanooga" in honor of the Cherokees.

Today, a $120-million renovation of the riverfront includes a generous allotment to commemorate the prior occupants of the land. A group that includes Cherokees in Tahlequah won the bid for an artistic interpretation. It showcases primarily shell artwork of pre-contact Cherokees and other Indians who lived on that soil. One of the giant shells—six feet in diameter—contains a giant circled cross, symbolizing the sun circle. According to the artists, 'it represents the Holy Sun's power, sent to the earth by the creator in the form of a sacred fire . . . it is said that the Cherokees will survive as long as the sacred fire burns.'

Chattanooga's RiverCity Company commissioned the art as well as the May, 2005 event celebrating the $120 million riverfront expansion. Organizers envisioned an event where 'returning to the waterfront' was celebrated with Chad Smith from Oklahoma and Michel Hicks, Chief of the Eastern Bank Cherokees, bringing torches of fire from a giant bonfire at the far side of the Tennessee River across from Chattanooga. In a reveresal of the Trail of Tears, the planners arranged for the chiefs to light 11 major fires on the Chattanooga side of the River. RiverCity planners also included the flight of an American bald eagle flying from the Market Street bridge over the audience and landing at the new Chattanooga Pier with a 25-voice Cherokee choir singing the National Anthem in Cherokee–joined later by a 300-voice Chattanooga choir. Plans included traditional games of stickball, making baskets, and playing flutes, and shooting dart guns, all a part of celebrating the revitalization of the riverfront area so cherished by the First Americans on the soil.

"The fact is, this was a very valuable spot," said Tom Decosimo, whose ancestor was a soldier in the removal. He notes that the Cherokees removed the Creeks a few hundred years earlier for the valuable location. He and his family own a large accounting firm in Chattanooga, and their offices overlook the city and the river.

As young boys, he and his brothers were taken by their grandmother and great aunts to care for the Brainerd Mission cemetery, the only remaining part of the mission complex today. A Kinko's and a Subway now sit at the site of the main building for the Brainerd Mission. A mall and several strip centers cover the remainder of the historical site. The area is mostly pavement and parking lots except for the cemetery, hidden by a small patch of trees.

The boys were told that others of their ancestors were kind to the Indians. Their grandmother founded the John Ross chapter of the Daughters of the American Revolution, which now owns the cemetery.

"Our ancestors helped usher them off. It's a fact," said Tom's brother Fred Decosimo. "I don't think I can pay anybody back for it. I don't think I should have to."

But both brothers concede that the removal was nothing short of "ethnic cleansing."

"It's like what they wanted to do in Bosnia, but they got away with it," said Tom.[5]

Most Chattanoogans, however, know little to nothing of the history of the area. They may have heard of John Ross—or at least they've heard of Ross's Landing and Rossville—and perhaps they are aware that the Trail of Tears started here.

Down the road a few miles, attempts are being made to better acquaint citizens with the story of the Cherokees. Red Clay, Tennessee, where the Cherokee Council met after being forced off New Echota, has been restored as a state park. In Rome, Georgia, the "Chieftain's Museum" showcases the splendid home of Major Ridge.

An hour from Chattanooga in Calhoun, Georgia, a 214-acre site provides a restored version of the capital city of New Echota. It is described as "a sort of Indian style Williamsburg" by a 1954 article detailing the restoration process.[6] In the 1930s, the area was a cotton field. A few women in Calhoun saw to it that a marker was placed in the field memorializing the site.

Reminiscent of his attempts to help the Cherokee Nation rise Phoenix-like out of the ashes, only Samuel Worcester's home remained standing, and it was quickly deteriorating.

Archeologists secured old surveyor's maps of the area and, along with old letters and clippings, were able to reconstruct the town. Today, several structures have been rebuilt, including both the upper and lower Council Houses, the Supreme Court Building, and the printing complex for the *Cherokee Phoenix*. A landmark next to Worcester's home is also restored, the spacious house of his neighbor Elias Boudinot.

The former house of John Ross still stands in Rossville. However, in the 1930s there was concern for its preservation when the owners contracted with a gas company to build a filling station in the front yard of the property.

The nine-room house was deteriorating. The newspaper said it looked like "an ordinary tenant shack." A knock on the door brought an overalled man to the door who lived in a small apartment in the rear. H.C. Bauer, a mechanic, paid $15 a month rent and cooked on a wood stove.

The mayor, who lived across the street, tried to stop the construction work for the gas station. And members of the D.A.R. protested. But they were told that the Rossville government lacked the zoning powers to stop the digging.

When both sides were convinced the city would not win the case—it was soon to be heard before the Georgia Supreme Court—the Rossville city fathers came up with a creative solution. They moved the entire house three hundred feet away to a safe location with better access to the public.[7]

Today, the John Ross House sits quietly in a small park behind a major grocery store in Rossville, Georgia, just five minutes from Chattanooga, Tennessee. Visitors can now view the area's oldest building. Office workers stop by to eat their lunch on picnic tables. Small children feed the ducks in the lake out front while their grandparents watch nearby.

That special sense of historical wonder is present when you observe the house in Rossville—the actual home where Ross and Ridge and many others deliberated, the home of Ross's grandfather who considered an alliance with Spain, and the place where many key decisions were made for the Cherokee Nation.

But there is still something lacking in the experience. The house doesn't sit in the actual spot where it was built.

Yes, it's the same structure. But that spiritual connection to the original soil is gone.

THE END

COMMENTS AND
ACKNOWLEDGEMENTS

The purpose of this book is to introduce the story of the Cherokees as well as the events and leaders behind their removal. Most Americans appear to be unfamiliar with the main plot line, much less the details of this saga, one of the most dramatic episodes in American history.

Great effort was taken to craft the story with character, plot, and conflict, taking full advantage of the inherent drama without comprising historical integrity. Readers looking for further scholastic contributions on the subject may find a few crumbs. However, this work is focused more on creative communication than on original research—although a few new items have been introduced, such as the poem Worcester wrote at age 18 and the pencil-scratched commentary below the statement of Allen Ross.

And it would be difficult to upstage the scholarship of the author to whom I am primarily indebted: Thurman Wilkins. His biography of the Ridges, *Cherokee Tragedy: The Ridge Family and the Decimation of a People*, displays a most welcome combination of academic mastery and literary acumen. I am also indebted to the work of Marion Starkey, *The Cherokee Nation*, whose eye for detail and humorous anecdotes shed important light on the role of the missionaries.

Wilkins and Starkey are the two authors most cited in this book. I attempted to name the original documents they cited for the most striking quotes. The others can be obtained from their footnotes.

The same is true for all citations from William McLoughlin, the impressive and most prolific of Cherokee scholars; Boudinot biographer Henry Gabriel, who provides the most detail on the Ridge and Boudinot marriages; and Robert Remini, the refreshing and indomitable biographer of Andrew Jackson. His last book on the man—*Andrew Jackson and His Indian Wars*, published in 2001—was a gift arriving in the nick of time, just after I initiated this project.

To avoid confusion and complexity for the reader, I liberated a small number of quotes from their unwieldy punctuation. While the letter of the law requires numerous brackets and ellipses, the spirit of this treatment called for an easy flowing narrative. In no case was a quote altered that changed the meaning in any sense.

Special thanks to those who agreed to be interviewed for this book. Thanks also to Krue Brock, Sam Smartt, Tom and Dorothy Worsham, Bill McClay, Eric Wertz, Daniel Westcott, Jon Warren, Dan Bockert, whose copy editing helped me correct hundreds of mistakes (but not all—some suggestions I could not execute with the software), and to Doug Daugherty, who planted the seed for this project.

Thanks to my sweet daughter Tabitha, eight, who is already writing about an Indian named "Scruffy" on my laptop, and to my son Jaime, six, whose smile brightens a day otherwise focused on past tragedies. My son also called me to a higher standard of digital backup after spilling on my laptop and frying the motherboard as I was nearing completion. (It was my fault. But nothing was lost, and the warranty covered it. Then I spilled a large cup of coffee on my typesetter's computer.)

Thanks, finally, to my father, who has been a tremendous support, and to my gifted mother, who never fails to encourage me toward creative and fulfilling endeavors. I certainly enjoyed this one.

BIBLIOGRAPHY

Adair, James, *Adair's History of the American Indians*. Ed. Samuel C. Williams. Johnson City, Tennessee, 1930.

Armstrong, Zella, *History of the First Presbyterian Church of Chattanooga*. Lookout Publishing Company, 1945.

Armstrong, Zella, *The History of Hamilton County and Chattanooga, Tennessee*. Chattanooga: The Lookout Publishing Company, 1931.

Arnold, Dean W. *Fighting Scots: A History of the American Spirit.* Unpublished Manuscript. PO Box 2053, Chattanooga, TN 37409, 1997.

Ballenger, T.L. "Death and Burial of Major Ridge," *The Chronicles of Oklahoma*, Vol. L1, Spring 1973, Num. 1, p. 100-105.

Bass, Althea, *Cherokee Messenger: A Life of Samuel Austin Worcester.* Norman: University of Oklahoma Press, 1936.

Bass, Dorothy C. "Gideon Blackburn's Mission to the Cherokees: Christianization and Civilization," *Journal of Presbyterian History*, Fall 1974.

Brown, Nancy Polson. Author's interview. Honey Creek, Oklahoma, November, 2003.

Buchanan, Patrick J. *A Republic, Not an Empire*. Washington D.C.: Regnery, 1999.

Buchanan, Patrick J. *The Great Betrayal.* Boston: Little, Brown and Company, 1998.

Butrick, Daniel, *The Journal of Rev. Daniel S. Butrick*. Park Hill, OK: Trail of Tears Association, Oklahoma Chapter, 1998.

Cherokee Heritage Center, Talequah, Museum Display.

Cherokee Heritage Center, Talequah, Special Collections.

Church, Mary P. "Elias Boudinot." *The Magazine of History*. XVII, No. 6, Dec. 1931: 209-19.

Dale, Edward E. and Gaston L. Litton, eds. *Cherokee Cavaliers*. Norman: University of Oklahoma Press, 1939.

Decosimo, Tom, and Fred Decosimo. Author's interview. Chattanooga, November 4, 2003.

Delly, Lillian, "Episode at Cornwall," *Chronicles of Oklahoma*. Ll, No. 4, Winter, 1973-74, p. 444-50.

Dippie, Brian W. *The Vanishing American*. Middletown, CT: Wesleyen University Press, 1982.

Eaton, Rachel Caroline, *John Ross and the Cherokee Indians*. Menasha, WI, 1921.

Ehle, John, *The Trail of Tears, The Rise and Fall of the Cherokee Nation*. New York: Doubleday, 1988.

Fellman, Michael, *Citizen Sherman: A Life of William Tecumseh Sherman*. New York: Random House, 1995.

Filler, Louis and Allen Guttman, eds. *Removal of the Cherokee Nation: Manifest Destiny or National Dishonor?* Boston, 1962.

Foreman, Carolyn Thomas, *Park Hill*. Muscogee: Starr Printing, 1948.

Foreman, Grant, *The Five Civilized Tribes*. Norman, 1934.

Foreman, Grant, *The History of Oklahoma*. Norman, University of Oklahoma Press, 1942.

Foreman, Grant, *Sequoia*. Norman, 1938.

Foreman, Grant, "The Murder of Elias Boudinot," *Chronicles of Oklahoma*. p. 19-24, XII, March, 1934.

Gabriel, Ralph Henry, *Elias Boudinot, Cherokee, & His America* Norman: University of Oklahoma Press, 1941.

Gilmer, George R. *Sketches of some of the first settlers of upper Georgia, of the Cherokees, and the author*. Baltimore: Genealogical Publishing Company, 1965.

Gold, Theodore S. *Historical Records of the Town of Cornwall, Litchfield County, Connecticut*. Hartford, 1877.

Govan, E. Gilbert and James W. Livingood, *The Chattanooga Country: 1540-1951*. New York: E.P. Dutton & Co. 1952.

Haywood, John, *The natural and aboriginal history of Tennessee, up to the first settlements therein by the white people, in the year 1768*. Nashville: Printed by G. Wilson, 1823.

Printed by G. Wilson, 1823.

Halbert, H.S. and T.H. Ball, *The Creek War of 1813-1814.* University of Alabama, 1969.

Independent, The, London, September 22, 2003.

John Ross House, Clipping file, Local History Department, Chattanooga-Hamilton County Bicentennial Library.

Johnson, Paul, *A History of the American People*. New York: HarperPerennial, 1998.

Kappler, Charles J. *Indian treaties, 1778-1883*. New York: Interland Pub. 1972. Reprint of *Indian affairs: laws and treaties*, v. 2, published in 1904 by Govt. Print. Office, Washington.

Kidd, Sam Watts, Curator, Cherokee Heritage Center. Author's interview. Talequah, October 13, 2003.

Kilpatrick, Jack F. and Anna Gritts Kilpartrick, *New Echota Letters*. Dallas: Southern Methodist University Press, 1968.

King, Duane H, ed. *The Cherokee Nation: A Troubled History*. Knoxville, 1979.

Livingood, James W. *A History of Hamilton County, Tennessee.* Memphis: Memphis State University Press, 1981.

Livingood, James W. and Norman O. Burns and Patrice H. Glass, *Chattanooga: An Illustrated History.* Sun Valley, CA: American Historical Press, 2001.

"Lobbying for survival: The chief of the Cherokee Nation positions his people for the next 100 years." *University of Georgia magazine*, Dec. 2002.

Lumpkin, Wilson, *The Removal of the Cherokees from Georgia*. Wormsloe, Georgia, 1907

Mails, Thomas E. *The Cherokee People: The Story of the Cherokees from the Earliest Origins to Contemporary Times*. Tulsa: Council Oak Books, 1992.

McLoughlin, William G. "The Mystery Behind Parson Blackburn's Whiskey." *Cherokee Ghost Dance*. Mercer University Press, 1984.

McLoughlin, William G. *Cherokees and Missionaries: 1789-1839*. New Haven: Yale University Press, 1984.

BIBLIOGRAPHY

McLoughlin, William G. *Cherokee Renascence in the New Republic*. Princeton: Princeton University Press, 1986.

McKenney, Thomas L. and James Hall, *History of the Indian Tribes of North America with Biographical Sketches and Anecdotes of the Principal Chiefs*. Philadelphia, 1836.

Mooney, James, "Cherokee River Cult." *Journal of American Folklore*. XIII. January-March 1900, p. 1-10.

Mooney, James, *Myths of the Cherokee; and, Sacred formulas of the Cherokees*. Nashville: Charles and Randy Elder, Booksellers, 1982.

Moulton, Gary E. *John Ross: Cherokee Chief*. Athens, GA, 1978.

Paul, the Apostle, The Epistle of Paul the Apostle to the Romans, The New Testament, King James Version (Authorized Version), 1611.

Pearce, Roy Harvey, *The Savages of America: A Study of the Indian and the Idea of Civilization*. Baltimore: Johns Hopkins Press, 1965.

Phillips, Joyce B. and Paul Gary Phillips. *The Brainerd Journal : A Mission to the Cherokees*, 1817-1823. Lincoln: University of Nebraska Press, 1998.

Prucha, Francis P. "Andrew Jackson's Indian Policy: A Reassessment." *Journal of American History*. XVI. No. 3. Dec. 1969, p. 527-39.

Purdue, Theda, *Cherokee Editor: The Writings of Elias Boudinot*. Knoxville: University of Tennessee Press, 1983.

Reid, John Phillip, *A Law of Blood: The Primitive Law of the Cherokee Nation*. New York, 1970.

Remini, Robert V. *Andrew Jackson and His Indian Wars*. New York: Viking, 2001.

Remini, Robert V. *Andrew Jackson and the Course of American Democracy*. New York: Harper & Row, 1977.

Remini, Robert V. *Andrew Jackson and the Course of American Empire*. New York: Harper & Row, 1984.

Remini, Robert V. *The Life of Andrew Jackson*. New York: Penguin Books, 1988.

Ridge, John Rollin, *Poems*. San Francisco: Henry Pavot & Company, 1868.

Rogers, Chief Charles Jahtlohi, M.D. *Cherokee Nation of Mexico*, Cherokeemexico.com/cultural-transformation.html.

Ross, John, *Papers*. Special Collections, Gilcrease Museum of History and Art, Tulsa.

Sheehan, Bernard W. *Seeds of Extinction: Jeffersonian Philanthropy and the American Indian*. Chapel Hill, 1973.

Smith, Chad, Principal Chief of the Cherokee Nation, Author's Interview. Talequah, October, 14, 2003.

Starkey, Marion L. *The Cherokee Nation*. New York: Russell & Russell, 1946.

Starr, Edward C. *History of Cornwall, Connecticut.* Cornwall, 1926.

Strickland, Rennard, *Fire and Spirits: Cherokee Law from Clan to Court*. Norman, OK, 1975.

Tennessee Encyclopedia of History & Culture. Nashville: Tennessee Historical Society and Rutledge Hill Press, 1998.

Tennessee Historical Quarterly, Vol. VI. Nashville: Tennessee Historical Society, 1965.

Thom, James Alexander, *Follow the River: A Novel Based on the True Story of Mary Ingles*. New York: Ballantine Books, 1981.

"The Trail Where They Cried," *Cherokee Observer On-Line*, April 8, 1998.

Walker, Robert Sparks, *Torchlight to the Cherokees, Johnson City, Tennessee*: The Overmountain Press, 1931.

Wilkins, Thurman, *Cherokee Tragedy: The Ridge Family and the Decimation of a People.* Norman: University of Oklahoma Press, 1986.

Wilson, John, *Chattanooga's Story*. Chattanooga: Chattanooga News-Free Press, 1980.

Woodward, Grace, *The Cherokees*. Norman: University of Oklahoma Press, 1963.

Worcester-Robertson Family Papers, Manuscripts Division, University of Tulsa Library.

Worcester, Samuel Austin, *Journal: 1825-1831*, Worcester-Robertson Family Papers, Manuscripts Division, University of Tulsa Library.

NOTES

PROLOGUE

[1] Sam Houston, *Writings of Sam Houston*, V, 1938-43, p. 520. Cited in Thurman Wilkins, *Cherokee Tragedy: The Ridge Family and the Decimation of a People*, 1986, p. 6.

CHAPTER 1: THE SECRET

[1] Thurman Wilkins, *Cherokee Tragedy*, 1986, p. 125; Edward C. Starr, *History of Cornwall, Connecticut*, 1926, Statement of Mrs. Ellen M. Gibbs, p. 154-7.

[2] Treaty of Holston, 1791; William McLoughlin, *Cherokee Renascence in the New Republic*, 1986, p. 329,154.

[3] Theodore S. Gold, *Historical Records of the Town of Cornwall, Litchfield County, Connecticut*, 1877, p. 351.

[4] Wilkins, *Cherokee Tragedy*, p. 102-7; *Brainerd Journal*, July 4, 1817.

[5] Ralph Henry Gabriel, *Elias Boudinot, Cherokee, & His America*, 1941, p. 52; Wilkins, p. 123-5.

[6] Statement of Ellen Gibbs in Starr, *History of Cornwall*, p. 155.

CHAPTER 2: THE MISSION

[1] Robert Sparks Walker, *Torchlight to the Cherokees*, 1931, p. 351; Wilkins, p. 116, 14-15.

[2] Robert V. Remini, *Andrew Jackson and His Indian Wars*, 2001, p. 64.

[3] James W. Livingood, *A History of Hamilton County, Tennessee*, 1981, p. 103; McLoughlin, *Cherokee Renascence*, p. 37; William G. McLoughlin, *Cherokees and Missionaries: 1789-1839*, 1984, p. 113.

[4] McLoughlin, *Cherokee Renascence*, p. 48, 251; McLoughlin, *Cherokees and Missionaries*, p. 112; *Brainerd Journal*, Sept. 9, 1817.

CHAPTER 3: THE SCANDAL

[1] Starr, p. 154-5

[2] Wilkins, p. 151; *Religious Intelligencer*, IV, p. 166f. cited in Gabriel, *Elias*

Boudinot, p. 54.

[3] John Rollin Ridge, *Poems*, p. 5; Wilkins, p. 131.

[4] Wilkins, p. 133.

[5] Gabriel, p. 61-2.

CHAPTER 4: THE LAND

[1] Gold, *Historical Records of the Town of Cornwall*, p. 353; Wilkins, p, 8-9; Remini, *Andrew Jackson and His Indian Wars*, p, 49; McLoughlin, *Cherokee Renascence*, p. 19.

[2] Paul Johnson, *A History of the American People*, p. 290.

[3] Roy Harvey Pearce, *The Savages of America: A Study of the Indian and the Idea of Civilization*, p. 19, 21, 67.

[4] McLoughlin, *Cherokee Renascence*, p. 208; Johnson, *History of the American People*, p. 294; Remini, p. 49.

[5] Wilkins, p. 40; McLoughlin, *Cherokee Renascence*, p. 126.

[6] H.S. Halbert and T.H. Ball, *The Creek War of 1813-1814*, p. 79-80, cited in Remini, p. 4.

[7] Peter Jones, *History of the Ojebway Indians*, p. 187-88, cited in Wilkins, p. 138.

[8] All quotes from Remini, p. 88-110.

[9] McLoughlin, *Cherokee Renascence*, p. 241-2, 261, 302-3.

CHAPTER 5: THE BRIBE

[1] Wilkins, p. 137, 144-5.

[2] McLoughlin, *Cherokee Renascence*, p. 306-7; *John Calhoun to Joseph McMinn,* April 22, 1823, cited in McLoughlin, p. 143, 313.

[3] Remini, p. 126.

[4] *American Eagle*, Sept. 27, 1824, cited in Gabriel, p. 64.

[5] *Niles Weekly Register*, XXVIII (July 9, 1825), cited in Wilkins, p. 146.

[6] *"Then and Now," Fort Smith Herald*, May 21, 1870, p. 2, cited in Wilkins, p. 147.

[7] Gold, Cornwall, p. 31-2.

NOTES

[8] Starr, p. 155; Gabriel, p. 63, 73.

[9] *Connecticut Journal*, Aug. 10, 1824, cited in Gabriel, p. 65.

[10] Gold, p. 276.

[11] Starr p. 156.

CHAPTER 6: THE LINGUIST

[1] *Spring Place Diary*, April 10, 1815, cited in Wilkins, 106.

[2] William B. Sprague, *Annals of the American Pulpit*, Vol. IV, 1858, p. 43f; Gideon Blackburn to Ashbel Green, Sept. 16, 1808; Blackburn to Jedidiah Morse, Nov. 10, 1807; all quotes cited in Dorothy C. Bass, "Gideon Blackburn's Mission to the Cherokees: Christianization and Civilization," *Journal of Presbyterian History*, Fall 1974, p. 203-226.

[3] McLoughlin, *Renascence*, p. 332.

[4] William Chamberlain, Journal, July 9, 1825; this and all previous quotes cited in McLoughlin, *Cherokees and Missionaries*, p. 199, 205-6, 208.

[5] Moody Hall to Jerermiah Evarts, Aug, 20, 1825, cited in McCoughlin, *Renascence*, p. 385.

[6] Marion L. Starkey, *The Cherokee Nation*, p. 62-3, 75-6.

[7] Isaac Proctor to Jeremiah Evarts, Feb. 4, 1828, cited in McLoughlin, *Missionaries*, p. 207-8.

[8] Bass, "Gideon Blackburn's Mission," p. 226; William McLoughlin, "The Mystery Behind Parson Blackburn's Whiskey," *Cherokee Ghost Dance*, p. 369ff.

[9] All previous quotes from Gambold correspondence cited in McLoughlin, *Missionaries*, p. 64, 66, 68.

[10] Starkey, *The Cherokee Nation*, p. 64.

[11] All previous quotes from McLoughlin, *Renascence*, p. 363, 382.

[12] Andrew Jackson to William Crawford, June 13, 1816, cited in Remini, p. 105.

[13] All quotes from Journal of Samuel Austin Worcester, Worcester-Robertson Family Papers, Manuscripts Division, University of Tulsa Library, p. 1-6.

[14] Gold, p. 276.

CHAPTER 7: THE RIOT

[1] Gibbs Statement, Starr, p. 155-6.

[2] Except for last paragraph, the remaining quotes in this chapter from Vaill Manuscripts, Stirling Library Yale, cited in Gabriel, p. 71-85.

[3] Starkey, p. 76; Moody Hall Diary, Aug. 9, 1825, Houghton Library, ABC, cited in Wilkins, p. 192-3.

CHAPTER 8: THE TRUCE

[1] McLoughlin, *Renascence*, p. 202, 269-70.

[2] All quotes from Roy Harvey Pearce, *The Savages of America*, p. 9, 11, 21-23, 29, 32, 42-3, 55.

[3] *Haywood's History of Tennessee*, p. 353-5; *Tennessee Historical Quarterly*, Vol. VI, p. 149; James W. Livingood, *History of Hamilton County, Tennessee*, p. 47-61; John Wilson, *Chattanooga's Story*, p. 6; *Tennessee Encyclopedia of History & Culture*, p. 583-4.

[4] *American State Papers: Indian Affairs*, Vol. 1, p. 13, 53, 61, cited in McLoughlin, *Renascence*, p. 35.

[5] Livingood, p. 44.

[6] Thomas L McKenney and James Hall, *History of the Indian Tribes of North America with Biographical Sketches and Anecdotes of the Principal Chiefs*, p. 398-421; Wilkins, *Cherokee Tragedy*, p. 25-6.

CHAPTER 9: THE INVENTION

[1] *Memoirs of John Quincy Adams*, ed. John Francis Adams, 1874, p. 229, cited in Wilkins, p. 154; John Ross and Cherokee Delegation to James Monroe, Jan. 19, 1824, cited in McLoughlin, *Renascence*, p. 306-7.

[2] All quotes cited in Wilkins, p. 155-8,

[3] Angie Debo, *The Road to Disappearance*, 1941, p. 88; Thomas McKenney to David Folsom, Dec. 13, 1827, both cited in McLoughlin, *Renascence*, p. 372, 375.

[4] Remini, p. 105, 126.

[5] Starkey, p. 91.

[6] Jones, *History of the Ojebway Indians*, p. 187-88, cited in Wilkins, p. 138; Gabriel, p. 103-4.

[7] Journal of Samuel Austin Worcester, p. 12.

NOTES

CHAPTER 10: THE CONSTITUTION

[1] *Cherokee Phoenix*, Aug. 20, 1828, cited in Wilkins, p. 199; Vaill Manuscripts, cited in Gabriel, p. 99.

[2] Chief Charles Jahtlohi Rogers, M.D. Cherokee Nation of Mexico, Cherokeemexico.com/cultural-transformation.html; Starkey, p. 7, 95.

[3] Starr, p. 38; *The Laws of the Cherokee Nation*, Talequah, p. 3-4, cited in McLoughlin, *Renascence*, p. 396.

[4] Wilkins, p. 153; Gabriel, p. 92; Starr, p. 278.

[5] Theda Purdue, *Cherokee Editor: The Writings of Elias Boudinot*, 1983, p. 68ff.

CHAPTER 11: THE OBSTACLES

[1] Wilkins, p. 165, 167.

[2] Theda Purdue, *Cherokee Editor: The Writings of Elias Boudinot*, 1983, p. 74-75.

[3] McLoughlin, *Renascence*, p. 390; Starkey, p. 105.

[4] Starkey, p. 106; McLoughlin, *Resascence*, p. 409.

[5] Joel Chandler Harris, *Georgia*, cited in Starkey, p. 109.

CHAPTER 12: THE PRESIDENT

[1] Robert V. Remini, *Andrew Jackson and the Course of American Empire*, Vol. 1, p. 7, 8; Patrick J. Buchanan, *A Republic, Not an Empire*, p. 82-85.

[2] Ibid, p. 87, 95.

[3] Ibid, p. 71.

[4] Robert V. Remini, *The Life of Andrew Jackson*, p. 43-4.

[5] Wilkins, p. 209-13; Starkey, p. 156.

CHAPTER 13: THE BLOOD LAW

[1] *Cherokee Phoenix*, Feb. 10, 1830 and Payne Papers, Ayer Collection, Newberry Library, both cited in Wilkins, 213, 209.

[2] Remini, *Andrew Jackson and His Indian Wars*, p. 235, 237, 242.

[3] Starkey, p. 124, Wilkins, p. 220-1.

4 Starkey, p. 120; McLoughlin, *Renascence*, p. 413, 417.

5 Starkey, p. 125.

6 McLoughlin, *Cherokees and Missionaries*, p. 252, 255fn; Starkey, p. 133-4.

7 *Cherokee Phoenix*, March 4, 1829, cited in Wilkins, p. 207.

8 McLoughlin, *Renascence*, p. 436; Starkey, p. 126-7.

CHAPTER 14: THE ARRESTS

1 *The Epistle of Paul the Apostle to the Romans,* The New Testament, King James Version, 1611; McLoughlin, Missionaries, p. 260-1; Wilkins, p. 226; Starkey, p. 134-6.

2 Richard Peters, ed. *The Case of the Cherokee Nation Against the State of Georgia*, p. 157-8, cited in Wilkins, p. 222.

3 Wilkins, 222-3.

4 Hugh Montgomery to John Forsyth, July 12, 1828, cited in McLoughlin, *Missionaries*, p. 331fn; Starkey, p. 139, 155, 159; McLoughlin, *Missionaries*, p. 258.

5 McLoughlin, *Missionaries*, p. 259-60; Starkey, p. 140.

6 Arrest and prison account taken primarily from Worcester's account in Robert Sparks Walker, *Torchlight to the Cherokees*, p. 264-276; Also, Starkey, p. 165; *Cherokee Phoenix*, Feb. 18, 1832, cited in Wilkins, p. 227; McLoughlin, *Missionaries*, p. 262.

CHAPTER 15: THE REBELLION

1 Gold, *History of Cornwall*, p. 351; Gabriel, p. 115.

2 George R. Gilmer, *Sketches of the First Settlers of Upper Georgia*, 1855, p. 330, cited in McLoughlin, *Missionaries*, p. 263; Starkey, p. 143, 180.

3 Toast scene from Marquis James, *Andrew Jackson: Portrait of a President*, p. 235 and Samuel Eliot Morison and Henry Steele Commager, *The Growth of the American Republic*, Vol. 1, p. 480-481, cited in Patrick J. Buchanan, *The Great Betrayal*, p. 150.

4 Background for the Nullification issue in relation to missionaries: McLoughlin, *Renascence*, p. 445-6 and *Missionaries*, p. 298-9; Buchanan, *The Great Betrayal*, p. 148-155; Robert V. Remini, *Andrew Jackson and the Course of American Freedom*, p. 276ff; Ronald N. Satz, *American Indian Policy in the Jacksonian Era*, 1975, p. 50ff; Wilkins, 231-2.

[5] Starkey, p. 166-7.

[6] *Cherokee Phoenix*, March 24, 1832, cited in Wilkins, p. 234.

[7] Starkey, p. 170, 192.

CHAPTER 16: THE REVERSAL

[1] Starkey, p. 164, 200; Jeremiah Evarts to Samuel Worcester, Feb. 1, 1831, cited in McLoughlin, *Missionaries*, p. 259.

[2] John B. McFerrin, *History of Methodism in Tennessee*, p. 373-4, cited in McLoughlin, *Missionaries*, p. 294; Starkey, p. 171, 198; Announcement of news and reaction: Wilkins, p. 235.

[3] Ronald N. Satz, *American Indian Policy in the Jacksonian Era*, 1975, p. 49; Starkey, p. 202.

[4] John Ridge to Stand Watie, April 6, 1832, Dale and Litton, eds. *Cherokee Cavaliers*, p. 8; Andrew Jackson to John Coffee, April 7, 1832, Coffee Papers, Tennessee Historical Society, cited in Remini, *AJ and His Indian Wars*, p. 257.

[5] Both quotes cited in Wilkins, p. 236-7.

[6] Remini, *AJ and His Indian Wars*, p. 46. He sources James Parton, *The Life of Andrew Jackson*, 1861, p. 227-229.

[7] Both quotes from Satz, *American Indian Policy in the Jacksonian Era*, p. 50-1.

[8] Starkey, p. 203; Ann Worcester to David Greene, Oct. 4, 1832, cited in McLoughlin, *Missionaries*, p. 298.

[9] Starkey, 204, 201; McLoughlin, *Missionaries*, p. 254.

[10] Worcester-Robertson Family Papers, Manuscripts Division, University of Tulsa Library.

[11] Worcester's Journal, p. 26; Samuel Worcester to "Brother and Sister" (probably James Orr), Feb. 1, 1833, Worcester-Robertson Family Papers, Manuscripts Division, University of Tulsa Library.

[12] McLoughlin, *Missionaries*, p. 298.

[13] Edwin A. Miles, "After John Marshall's Decision," *Journal of Southern History*, 39, 1973, p. 541, cited in McLoughlin, *Renascence*, p. 446.

CHAPTER 17: THE COLLAPSE

[1] John Ross to Elizur Butler, March 1833, cited in McLoughlin, *Missionaries*, p. 299; John Ross to the Cherokees, April 14, 1831, cited in Remini, *AJ and His Indian Wars*, p. 262;

[2] See chapter 8, note 3.

[3] Wilkins, p. 249, 252; Starkey, p. 216.

[4] John Ridge to John Ross, Feb. 2, 1833, Ross Papers, Gilcrease Institute, Tulsa, 33-2; Silas Dinsmore to John Ross, March 1, 1830, Ross Papers, Gilcrease Institute; On McDonald and Spain: McLoughlin, *Renascence*, p. 25.

[5] Remini, *AJ and Indian Wars*, p. 263-5; Wilkins, p. 267.

[6] Starkey, p. 192-3; Wilkins, p. 246.

[7] Wilkins, p. 263-5.

[8] Ibid, p. 269, 285.

[9] *Cartersville (GA) Courant*, March 26, 1885, cited in Wilkins, p. 287.

[10] Gabriel, p. 157-8; Wilkins, p. 296.

[11] Ibid.

[12] Grace Steele Woodward, *The Cherokees*, p. 193, cited in Wilkins, p. 292.

CHAPTER 18: THE TEARS

[1] James Mooney, *Myths of the Cherokees*, 1900, p. 130; Cherokee Heritage Center, Talequah, Museum Display 11B; Starkey, p. 288, 290.

[2] *The Journal of Rev. Daniel S. Butrick*, Trail of Tears Association, p. 6, 10, 26, 32-3, 36-7; Starkey, p. 294-5; Woodward, *The Cherokees*, p. 217-18; Wilkins, p. 323; Captain Phelps Journal, June 22, 1838, Cherokee Heritage Center, Museum Display.

[3] Wilkins, p. 328; Remini, p. 269; Mooney, *Myths of the Cherokee*, p. 130.

CHAPTER 19: THE AVENGER

[1] Butler to Greene, Aug. 2, 1838, cited in Wilkins; John Rollin Ridge, *Poems*, p. 7; Wilkins, p. 322.

[2] Wilkins, p. 237.

[3] Worcester to Greene, June 26, 1839, cited in Gabriel, p. 178; Grant Foreman, "The Murder of Elias Boudinot," *Chronicles of Oklahoma*, , March 1934; Wilkins, p. 334-9; John Rollin Ridge, *Poems*, p. 7-8; *Niles National Register,* LVI, Aug. 3, 1839, p. 362, cited in Wilkins, p. 335.

[4] John Rollin Ridge, *Poems*, p. 7-8.

[5] Wilkins, p. 338.

[6] Starkey, p. 313-318; Wilkins, p. 340-343.

[7] Author's interview with Chad Smith, Principal Chief of the Cherokee Nation, Talequah, Oct. 14, 2003.

EPILOGUE: WHO BETRAYED THE CHEROKEES?

[1] Paul Johnson, *The History of the American People*, p. 351.

[2] Wilkins, 340, 251fn; Grant Foreman, *A History of Oklahoma*, p. 143, cited in Wilkins, p. 251.

[3] Wilkins, 292-3; Ross to Cherokees, April 14, 1831, cited in Remini, *AJ and His Indian Wars*, p. 262.

[4] McLoughlin, *Renascence*, p. 450-1; Remini, *AJ and His Indian Wars*, p. 271.

[5] Author's interview with Sam Watts Kidd, Curator, Cherokee Heritage Center, Oct. 13, 2003.

[6] Wilkins, p. 289, 293.

[7] Starkey, p. 297; Remini, *AJ and His Indian Wars*, p. 270.

[8] "The Trail Where They Cried," *Cherokee Observer On-Line,* April 8, 1998.

[9] Interview with Sam Watts Kidd; Payne Papers, Ayer Collection, Newberry Library, cited in Wilkins, p. 209.

[10] Wilson Lumpkin, *The Removal of the Cherokees from Georgia*, 1907, p. 192; Starkey, p. 284; Edward Schwarze, *History of the Moravian Missions among Southern Indian Tribes of the United States*, p. 191, cited in Wilkins, p. 339.

[11] Statement of Allen Ross, 1891, John Ross Papers, 90-1, Gilcrease Institute, Tulsa.

[12] *Cherokee Phoenix*, Dec. 7, 1833, cited in Wilkins, p. 258-9; Starkey, p. 207-212; McLoughlin, Renascence, p. 448.

[13] Samuel Worcester to James Orr, Feb. 1, 1833, Worcester-Robertson Family Papers, Manuscripts Division, University of Tulsa Library; Starkey, p. 248.

[14] Lobbying for survival: The chief of the Cherokee Nation positions his people for the next 100 years, University of Georgia magazine, Dec. 2002; Remini, *AJ and Indian Wars*, p. 238, 5; Andrew Jackson: Message to Congress, Dec. 3, 1833, cited in McLoughlin, *Renascence*, p. 449; Ibid, 449 footnote.

[15] Richard Drinnon, *Facing West*, p. 179-80, cited in McLoughlin, *Renascence*, p. 449.

[16] Remini, *The Life of Andrew Jackson*, p. 215; Remini, *AJ and His Indian Wars*, p. 281, 228, 299fn; Johnson, *History of the American People*, p. 351.

[17] Remini, *AJ and His Indian Wars*, p. 299, 238; Marquis James, *The Life of Andrew Jackson*, p. 776, cited in Patrick J. Buchanan, *A Republic, Not an Empire*, p. 115.

[18] Remini, *The Life of Andrew Jackson*, p. 219; Remini, *AJ and His Indian Wars*, p. 281.

[19] Remini, *The Life of Andrew Jackson*, p. 215; McLoughlin, *Renascence*, p. 448; A. De Tocqueville, *Democracy in America*, I 353ff, cited in Johnson, *A History of the American People*, p. 352.

AUTHOR'S POSTSCRIPT: REMEMBERING THE BETRAYAL

[1] Grant Foreman, "Death and Burial of Major Ridge," *The Chronicles of Oklahoma*, Vol. L1, Spring 1973, Num. 1, p. 104-5.

[2] Author's interview with Nancy Polson Brown, Honey Creek, Oklahoma, November, 2003.

[3] Author's interview with Chad Smith, Principal Chief of the Cherokee Nation, Talequah, Oct. 14, 2003.

[4] *The Independent*, London, Sept. 22, 2003.

[5] Author's interview with Tom and Fred Decosimo, Chattanooga, Nov. 4, 2003.

[6] This unattributed news clipping hangs in a frame on the wall at the New Echota Center. The curator there believes it comes from an Atlanta paper in 1954.

[7] *Chattanooga Times*, Jan. 12, 1936, p. 3 and *Chattanooga Times Free Press*, March 1, 2001, p. B2, from John Ross House clipping file, Local History Department, Chattanooga-Hamilton County Bicentennial Library.

INDEX

ABOUT THE AUTHOR

Dean Arnold is a journalist, author, and publisher in Chattanooga, Tennessee. He was born in California where his great-grandparents located in the 1920s after making the Oklahoma Run in the Cherokee Strip in 1893.

Arnold has written an historical novel on the Scottish Reformation and its impact on American Independence. An avid local historian, he is currently finishing a broad social history of Chattanooga that includes 50 interviews with leading multi-generational families and heirs to the Coca-Cola bottling fortune.

He graduated from Covenant College on Lookout Mountain with an emphasis in history and philosophy—but has learned a good bit of late from John Chrysostom.

His avocations include jazz clubs, golf, and good cigars. Since these are too expensive, he spends more time sipping coffee at Greyfriar's or poring over old documents for gems related to genealogy and local history. But his favorite activity is late-night conversation with good friends over borrowed tobacco.

America's Trail of Tears resulted from the mysterious murders, ironies, and unanswered questions that emerged after local research into early Chattanooga history. It required an entire book to tell this amazing episode in Cherokee history. To contact the author with comments or questions, email him at dean@cdc.net

QUICK ORDER FORM

Please send me _____ copies of *America's Trail of Tears*.
  (Cost is $19.95. Shipping is $3.00 for one book.
  $2.00 for each additional book.)

Please send me _____ copies of CD Audio Book.
  (Under title *Cherokee Betrayal*. Same price as book)

Name: _____

Address: _____

City/State/Zip: _____

Phone (optional but helpful): _____

Email (optional but helpful): _____

Make all checks payable to Dean Arnold.

Mail order with check to:

Dean Arnold
P.O. Box 2053
Chattanooga, TN 37409

To phone in an order: 423-595-3621
To email in an order: dean@cdc.net